MW00462632

COMING OF AGE IN EL SALVADOR

Verdada Press (comingofagebook.com)

Printed by CreateSpace

Winship, Jim
Coming of Age in El Salvador

ISBN 978-0-692-20665-2

Cover design by Jenny McGee
Layout design by Kirsten Zimmer and Hope Winship
Graphic design by Julie Esenther

For Virginia Quintana, the hardest working person I know,
whose curiosity to understand the intersections between
youth, gender, and migration is a constant inspiration

Table of Contents

Preface

This book is about young adults who live simultaneously in both a globalized world and a small country in Central America. That country, El Salvador, fosters strong family connections and has great beauty, yet poses significant challenges and offers too few opportunities. In this book, I am trying to display how the country's positive aspects as well as its limitations and dangers affect the lives and choices of young Salvadorans. The tension between their dreams and goals and current confining realities intensifies the struggle between finding a meaningful life in El Salvador or leaving families and friends to emigrate to the United States.

Coming of Age in El Salvador draws on the research that my colleague Virginia Quintana and I have conducted in El Salvador on youth, as well as on the research of others. It also incorporates my experiences and reflections over a period of four decades— the two years I spent in El Salvador as a Peace Corps Volunteer in the early 1970s, half a year as a Fulbright Scholar in 2005, and twice-yearly trips to El Salvador since then. Our studies and the "Stories" chapter in this book profile young adults who come from the urban areas in and around San Salvador, from the coast, from a small city and remote rural communities in the west-central part of the country, and from a rural area and small town in the northwest part of the country. I am aware of the degree to which the challenges and opportunities that young Salvadorans face vary greatly from place to place, and how this book cannot capture the breadth of experience in coming of age in El Salvador.

The book starts with "Living Between," an overview of the ways that the lives of Salvadoran youth and young adults are in flux. There is a section on context, with chapters on the geography and the history of the country. These chapters are not specifically about youth and young adults, but provide information on the country.

The chapter "Stories" is comprised of accounts by individual Salvadorans, for the most part drawn from interviews I have conducted with youth over the past few years. Rather than use pieces from the interviews to illustrate points in the chapters, I wanted their stories to stand on their own. Following these is a section on forces affecting youth: family, migration, education, the economy, and violence. The conclusion looks again at the choices youth have for leaving or staying, and at how some are choosing to contribute to the country and its future. Because remittances—money sent home to families from Salvadorans working abroad—are an integral part of Salvadoran life, there is an appendix on this, along with another on U.S. immigration laws.

My intent for the book is not to downplay the very real obstacles that youth face in El Salvador as they come of age. I want to show both the challenges and the resources that youth have as they make decisions that will affect both their future and the country's future.

All of the profits from the sale of this book are going to help organizations that support youth and young adults: Glasswing, a non-profit that provides education and inquiry-based afterschool programs for youth (www.glasswing.org), and scholarships at the Universidad Panamericana de El Salvador (upan.edu.sv).

1

Introduction: Living Between

If you had the power to see into the places in the country of El Salvador where teens and young adults live, you would see young people attending high school and college in greater numbers than ever before. You would see some young adults struggling to find work and others, with steady and somewhat sufficient income, forming families. You would see many youth in daily communication with parents, siblings, or other relatives living in the United States. If you could listen to their conversations with parents and friends, you would note that many of them are considering going to the U.S., some through legal procedures of family reunification, and others hoping to cross the border between the U.S. and Mexico without being stopped.

As I started to write this book, I remembered what the novelist Walter Mosley said when he came a few years ago to speak at the university where I teach. In his talk, he mentioned that he had just come back from Ghana, where he had met with a group of young people. He told them: "The world knows little about your situation, and cares even less."

I think that the same is true for youth in El Salvador. To begin with, many people in the United States would have trouble placing El Salvador on a map of Latin America. It is located in Central

America, about halfway down. It borders Guatemala, Honduras, and Nicaragua. Guatemala, Honduras, and El Salvador are referred to as the Northern Triangle of Central America, and those three countries have much in common.

As to the importance of knowing about youth in El Salvador, I believe that there is value in understanding how people in other parts of the world conduct their lives. There are similarities between youth in El Salvador and in the United States (like social media and youth culture) and differences (job opportunities, family structures, migration). Understanding how a young person in El Salvador navigates the journey from adolescence to adulthood can offer a fresh perspective on life for someone of the same age in the United States.

I will be making comparisons between the experiences of young Salvadorans and youth in the United States. Their experiences in many respects are not that dissimilar, as El Salvador is not of those remote places in the world that still have centuries-old paths to adulthood involving children gradually accepting the work and family patterns of their parents and grandparents.

Coming of age is the process of becoming an adult, a transition that involves "living between." When I visualize "living between," I think of being neither here nor there, like the instant in which one is jumping over a puddle. "Between" can mean "being in flight" or "being stuck." Both meanings can apply at different points in time.

I think there are four commonalities in living between for youth in the U.S. and those in El Salvador. I would maintain that there are additional ways in which Salvadoran youth are in a time of transition.

Firstly, those youth still in adolescence in El Salvador, like teens everywhere, are in that transition into adulthood. As significant as the physical changes that occur in puberty are the changes in brain development. Scanning techniques have shown that the maturation of the brain from childhood to adulthood is uneven, with the areas that regulate critical thinking and impulsivity lagging behind other cognitive growth.

Secondly, youth everywhere face uncertainty as they contemplate how to find their place in the world. In Zygmunt Bauman's words, they (like the rest of us) are living in "liquid times." Until recently, in developing countries like El Salvador, as one grew up one would follow well-known and expected patterns that provided a rather limited set of what Arjun Appadurai calls "possible lives."

As the National Research Council puts it in *Growing Up Global: The Changing Transitions to Adulthood in Developing Countries*: "Globalization per se is not new, but what is new is the speed, scale, scope, and complexity of this process." The same report states that the transition to adulthood has transformed at the beginning of the 21st century. Young people in developing countries are coming of age in a world that is not only rapidly changing, but also with "simultaneous changes in technology, economics, culture, politics, demographics, the environment, and education." Advances in technology—email, Facebook, Skype, and low-cost cellular phones—facilitate communication across national borders. Migration worldwide "is no longer simply from the farm to the city, but across international boundaries," and in some cases between continents.

The third commonality between youth in the U.S. and in El Salvador is that in both cases, their worlds are far different than the ones their parents faced as adolescents and this can create a generation gap. It has been said, "Every generation is a separate culture." When a young person's experience is far different than that of his or her parents, the parents are less able to understand and provide guidance. I see a greater "generation gap" between youth and their parents in El Salvador compared to the United States. Many Salvadoran parents grew up during the country's civil war. By the end of the war in 1992, 30% of Salvadorans over the age of 14 had never attended school, and only a third had more than a 6th-grade education.

Young women in El Salvador see the future differently than how it was seen in the past, and do not want to necessarily follow in their mothers' and grandmothers' footsteps. As Carlos Ramos notes, in answering the question "What do you see yourself doing in five years?," only 13.7 percent of female respondents stated that they would be only dedicated to their family. Almost 35 percent stated that they would be working as an employee, with half that number saying that they would be self-employed (17.7%), and essentially the same number saying that they would continue with their studies (17.0%).

The generation gap is magnified in El Salvador by the prevalence of grandparents raising their grandchildren, as the children's parents are living in other countries. The doubling of the generation gap—from children to grandparents—did not become apparent to me until two Salvadoran professionals in their late 20s/early 30s described the great difference between their perceptions of the world and those of their grandparents who raised them.

A fourth area in which there is some degree of commonality in both countries is that increasing numbers of youth do not move directly from adolescence to the adult world of marriage and the kind of work they will do through their lifetime. One indicator of this is the age of first marriage, which has increased over a generation in the United States and now is over 27 years. In El Salvador, the increase in the age of first marriages has been much more rapid—from an average age of 18.2 years in 1996 to 23 years in 2012. Rising numbers of students attending college in both countries contributes to youth being in the stage that psychologist Jeffrey Arnett has described as "emerging adulthood," an extended period between being an adolescent and fully adopting adult roles, in which youth become more independent and explore various life possibilities.

As Brown, Larson, and Saraswathi point out in *The World's Youth: Adolescence in Eight Regions of the Globe*, the forces of globalization "are being refracted through distinct circumstances and cultural systems," leading to differences in adolescence and emerging adulthood between countries.

I believe that there are at least three ways in which Salvadoran youth and young adults live between that do not apply to many coming of age in the United States.

The first difference is that for Salvadoran youth *always* on the horizon is the possibility of migrating. A third of Salvadorans live outside their country, mostly in *Los United*, as it has been referred to. Everyone knows people who have emigrated, and cell phones, email, and social media maintain and strengthen those distant connections. In situations where one's parents have become U.S. citizens or are permanent residents, the parents can petition to bring their children in legally (this is a process that can take years— see Appendix B on U.S. immigration laws). When there are not legal ways to migrate, the family will often sell what they have or a relative will pay up to $10,000 for a *coyote* or smuggler to get the person across borders to the U.S.

As I talk to Salvadorans about migration, in addition to asking if they have thought about going to the United States, I also often ask: "Why do you stay here?" On the surface, it's a strange question to be asking—why stay in your home country, your own country? I ask this question in focus groups, in talking with taxi drivers, and in conversation with Salvadorans that I know or meet. If I were to ask that question to my neighbors or co-workers in Wisconsin, I would expect a pause before a reply—it's not a question that many people in the United States are used to answering, or even thinking about.

A second difference between youth in these two countries, tied into the phenomenon of mass migration, is that many Salvadoran youth benefit from remittances sent from parents or other family members working abroad.

Youth receiving money from abroad have the "stuff" that is common in the United States—computers, tablets, and particularly cell phones. Cell phone usage is greater than 100% in El Salvador (some people have more than one), and cell phones reach rural areas where there have never been phone lines. I can call the United States from El Salvador for less than ten cents a minute on a pre-paid cell phone. One does not pay for incoming calls in El Salvador; many families in rural and poor areas use their cell phones largely to receive calls from the United States.

Through technology, contact with family members living abroad tends to be continuous. In the study *One Family, Two Countries* that I conducted in 2005 with youth who had one or more parent(s) living and working in the United States, almost all of them said they talked at least once every eight days with the absent mother or father. Teens and young adults also stay in contact with family and friends increasingly through the Internet. As of late 2012,

24.5% of the country used Facebook. I see the familiar Facebook screen when I walk through coffee shops and restaurants there. Rebeca, who speaks in the "Stories" chapter, graduated from a small high school in 2005, with 42 in her graduating class. More than half are now in the U.S., and the graduates are in constant contact with each other through Facebook.

A third difference between the lives of most young Salvadorans and the lives of most young people in the United States is the degree to which violence and personal security are constant concerns. As explained in the chapter "Violence," El Salvador's murder rate puts it in the top third of the most dangerous countries in the world, and recently it was much higher. While there are cities in the U.S. with higher murder rates per capita than the country of El Salvador, my experience in both countries is that there are continual worries about personal safety in a far higher percentage of communities in El Salvador than in the United States. In many parts of the United States, concerns about personal safety are not as ever-present as they are for many Salvadorans.

A fourth (and obvious) difference between young Salvadorans and those in the United States is the country in which they are growing up. In the United States, we tend to lump together "Third World" or "developing" countries in Africa, Southeast Asia, and Latin America. While El Salvador is a country with poverty and other serious problems, living there is not the same as living in the poorest countries in the world. Also, when one looks at the country through measures other than economic well-being, a more complicated picture emerges of life in El Salvador.

One indication of El Salvador's "middling" position in the world came from The Economist Intelligence Unit (EIU), a sister company of the magazine *The Economist*. They used current indicators and economic data to forecast which countries provide the best opportunities for a healthy, safe, and prosperous life in the years ahead. In their forecast, El Salvador ranked 62nd out of the top 80 countries to be born in (out of the 195 countries with political recognition). This ranking was slightly worse than Iran's and Lithuania's, but slightly better than the Philippines' and India's.

El Salvador's middle position is also represented in the graph on page 10, which shows a comparison with three other countries:

the United States; Argentina, the second largest economy in South America; and Uganda, a poor African country.

On life expectancy, years of education, and average annual income, El Salvador does not compare favorably to either the United States or Argentina. But there is more to life than annual income, education levels, and life expectancy. In 2011, the Gallup polling organization measured positive emotions in 148 countries by asking people five questions: whether they experienced a lot of enjoyment the day before the survey; whether they felt respected, well-rested, laughed and smiled a lot; and whether they did or learned something interesting.

In the poll, El Salvador ranked 3rd highest on happiness and positive emotions (Singapore, which ranked 26th best out of 187 countries in the United Nations Development Fund Human Development Index ranking, came in as the least happy place in the world). When we add the rankings on happiness (or positive emotions) to the table of the four countries, a more complicated picture of El Salvador's place in the world emerges.

I continually ask Salvadorans how it is that residents in this highly congested and relatively poor country rank near the top of a happiness index (and have ranked very highly in similar surveys over the years). I have asked waiters, professionals, small business owners, a Cabinet Minister, and many others this question.

Many times people are stumped by the question. What comes up most often is that Salvadorans are nice, that they are welcoming, and that this attitude permeates their lives. Elena, a German in her mid-twenties who had volunteered in El Salvador for nine months a few years earlier, told me about getting depressed when she moved back to Germany: "In El Salvador, there is so much warmth in the people," she said. "They are friendly, hugging you because they are glad to see you again. In Germany, even around my family and friends, I missed this; I felt lonely."

One Salvadoran business owner, who also owns businesses in the U.S., said: "Salvadorans are hard-working—in the U.S. I hear people in business saying that they would rather hire Salvadorans than other Latinos, but it's more than that. We are always looking for a way around problems, a way to get by or get ahead. We are a positive people."

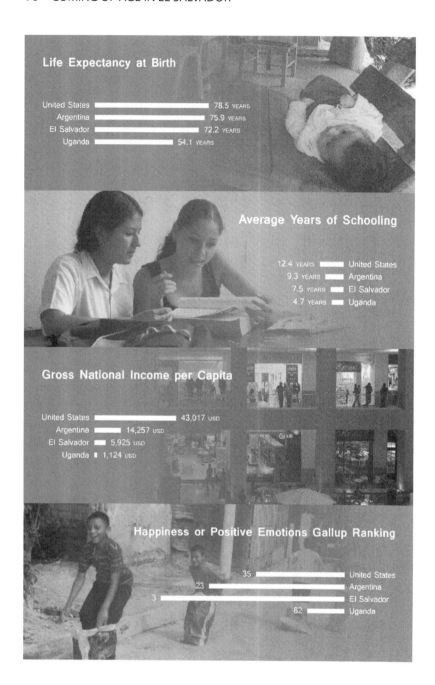

Life Expectancy at Birth

United States	78.5 YEARS
Argentina	75.9 YEARS
El Salvador	72.2 YEARS
Uganda	54.1 YEARS

Average Years of Schooling

12.4 YEARS	United States
9.3 YEARS	Argentina
7.5 YEARS	El Salvador
4.7 YEARS	Uganda

Gross National Income per Capita

United States	43,017 USD
Argentina	14,257 USD
El Salvador	5,925 USD
Uganda	1,124 USD

Happiness or Positive Emotions Gallup Ranking

35	United States
23	Argentina
3	El Salvador
82	Uganda

Another person who responded was a waiter at an ocean-front hotel who said: "It's family—it's living with family." Family is exceedingly important in El Salvador. I asked three Salvadorans (aged 25 to 35) who had decided to come home after living in the United States what they missed about their home country. All three of them mentioned family. Now, I know that family is important to most of us, but most Americans I know don't spend as much time with family members as Salvadorans do. One musician who had lived in the U.S. said: "On Sundays I got so lonely." Sundays are family days, and the rest of the week can be so as well. A young professional who had moved back to El Salvador from the U.S. said that she chose to live by herself instead of with family members, which is common if one is unmarried; living alone was the only way she could have any time for herself.

Responding to the question of why Salvadorans rank so high on a happiness index, one friend remarked: "Death is always around the corner here." There is the legacy of death from the civil war and the present danger of being a casualty of gang violence—El Salvador has ranked as high as second in the world for homicides per capita. Also, as I point out in Chapter 2, "Geography," the chances of dying from natural disasters are much higher in El Salvador than in the United States.

There is a harshness as well as a beauty to living in El Salvador. According to my friend Eva, if one realizes that one could die tomorrow, it is good to have an attitude of happiness and appreciation for life today. Elena, who had been hit hard with reverse culture shock when she returned home to Germany, said: "In Germany and the United States, one can assume that life will just go on—there's a sense of security. In El Salvador, you appreciate your life every day." In the words of another Salvadoran: "*Jodido pero contento*" (screwed but happy).

While the research on what leads to happiness is not conclusive (research is difficult because we do not have an agreed-upon definition of "happiness"), a number of studies have found that being happy in your day-to-day life is different and perhaps more important than being happy about your life in general. When Dr. Edward Diener, one of the leading researchers on happiness, and his colleagues separated subjective well-being into life evaluation and positive and negative feelings, they found that fulfillment of psychological needs was a stronger predictor of feelings than was income.

Thinking about how one's day-to-day positive interactions affect one's sense of being happy, I understand how El Salvador's high ranking on the happiness index resonates with me personally. I feel something different when I am in this small Central American country. Waiting in Atlanta to board a flight to San Salvador the last time I went down, I heard the laughter of the passengers in line behind me. Salvadorans, I thought, smiling. I know that I laugh more in El Salvador than when I am in the United States, and this has been the case since my Peace Corps days. I keep going back to El Salvador because I believe my knowledge, skills, language, and experience are useful in the country. But it is also true that the people and my enjoyment of being there keep pulling me back.

I don't want to imply that because Salvadorans rank high on a happiness scale that this means changes are not necessary, or that the poverty and lack of opportunities should be minimized.

If we return to the observation of the novelist Walter Mosley about the lack of interest in the circumstances of youth in the developing world, one can ask: "Why should readers in the United States care about Salvadorans aged 15–29 as they navigate adolescence and become adults?" The experiences of youth and young adults in El Salvador bear out the assertion that we live in an increasingly interconnected world. In his book *Six Degrees*, the mathematician Duncan Watts advocates for understanding geographically distant events: "Just because something seems far away, and just because it happens in a language you don't understand, doesn't make it irrelevant. ... To misunderstand this is to misunderstand the first great lesson of the connected age: we may all have our own burdens, but like it or not, we must bear each other's burdens as well."

Bearing another's burdens is one way of looking at it; one can also say that the actions of governments and individuals in both El Salvador and the United States affect each other. As I describe in the chapter on "Violence," the problem with Salvadoran gangs and violence has its roots in decisions made by the U.S. government to deport gang members originally from El Salvador who were living in Los Angeles after fleeing the civil war in their home country. Another clear example of the interconnectedness of youth in El Salvador and the United States is immigration. El Salvador, the smallest country in Latin America, has more of its populace living in the United States than any country other than Mexico, and about half of the immigrants are undocumented. The role that migration plays in the life plans of young Salvadorans has consequences for immigration policies in the U.S.

Additionally, actions by those in the United States and elsewhere in the world can contribute to conditions where Salvadoran youth can find a way to effectively stay in and contribute to their country.

CONTEXT

2

Geography

The Spanish philosopher José Ortega y Gasset wrote: "*Yo soy yo y mi circumstancia,*" which can be translated as "I am myself and my surroundings/circumstances." The context we live in has an impact on our daily lives, in many ways shaping the lives of young people coming of age. Knowing something of El Salvador—its size, density, the beauty and precariousness of the natural environment—helps us better understand the context in which young people there are coming of age.

Let's start with the size of the country. The Chilean poet Gabriela Mistral, the first Latin American to win the Nobel Prize in Literature, described El Salvador as the "*pulgarcito de America,*" the "little thumb of America." El Salvador is often referred to as "*el rinconcito del mundo,*" the "small corner of the world." When I Googled "*rinconcito,*" I found at least 20 restaurants by that name serving Salvadoran food, from Statesboro, Georgia to Vancouver to Lexington, Nebraska.

The country is small, a little over 8,000 square miles in area. It is 1/20th the size of the state of California, 1/10th the size of Kansas or Minnesota, 1/7th the size of Georgia, and slightly smaller than Massachusetts. To cross the country the longest way on the four-lane Pan American highway, one only travels 221 miles. From San

Salvador, the capital, with a good vehicle one can go for a weekend to any part of the country.

This smallness can affect the cultural concept of distance within a country. For example, last year, one of the staff members at the Universidad Panamericana asked me if I could take a package to a family member in the U.S. "Where does she live?" I asked. "Hyattsville, Maryland" was the answer. From where I live in Wisconsin, it is 806 miles to Hyattsville.

Not only is El Salvador the smallest country in the Americas (not counting islands), it also has the highest population density. With 853 persons per square mile, it is almost three times as crowded as Guatemala, the country with the next highest population density. El Salvador has 10 times the population density of the United States.

A distant and panoramic view of the mountains gives the impression of untouched tropical forest. However, a detailed map of the country that includes the dirt roads actually resembles a diagram of capillary veins. A closer look at most of the steep and rock-strewn mountainsides reveals neatly divided tiny farming plots where many in the rural population farm two to three acres of rented land, typically growing corn and beans for consumption. It seems as if every dirt road leads to communities of several hundred to several thousand families, and every path leads to a home or a farmer's field.

In a place this small and dense, it is paradoxical how inaccessible some parts of the country are. In rural, often mountainous areas where the roads are not paved, making your way can be an exceedingly slow process. In conducting interviews for a documentary in 2005, we drove from the city of Ilobasco to the village of Huertas in the rainy season. It was a little over a 9-mile trip, and it took us 45 minutes to get there in a good four-wheel-drive vehicle.

Another example of how remote some communities can be comes from Clayton Kennedy, who as a Peace Corps Volunteer lived in El Higueral, a community of just under 200 in Chalatenango, close to Honduras. He described the process of getting there this way:

> You have to ford the river six times and hike up a mountain cowpath to reach my village.

> Seriously: it's a seventy-minute tramp that would rate as "moderately strenuous" in a U.S. guidebook. And it would be there, in

the book, because it's gorgeous: lacing through stands of banana and mango trees, grazing by ancient cows with curled horns, descending into dark, musty jungles before cresting out into panoramic vistas of El Salvador's north-central highlands.

But this is not a trail that people take on the weekend to grab some fresh air and exercise Pooch. No, this is the path my villagers use to get home. And anything you can picture yourself unloading from the trunk or back seat of your car after pulling into your driveway, well, the people here strap it on their back, or balance it on their head…and start walking.

I've been told that during the six months of rainy season the river grows ferocious enough to steal your baby, so you're forced to say a prayer and twinkle-toe-it across the less-broken boards of the "hammock bridge." I crossed the bridge during dry season and admit that it's already prayer-worthy.

I can also confirm that the trail is steep: your back begins to itch with sweat about sixty meters after leaping off the bus, and by the time you stumble out into our dusty plaza you've drenched your shirt and the top quarter of your pants. The first villagers who see you will smile gently and ask if you've been swimming.

And you'll smile back, knowing that they've hiked the trail hundreds of times before….

There is not much work in the community described above. For example, one person in El Higueral works as a health promoter in his community and the surrounding area. Another works in a range of rural communities as an educator and advocate for the government-funded *Red Solidaria* (Solidarity Network). One man goes into San Salvador for part of the week, where he works as a police officer. Many men and women hike to ranches and farms for daily wage labor, which is seasonal.

Commuting to urban areas for work from this community on a daily basis is not possible. The hike described above can take up to two hours to get to a road. Then one can catch a bus, and buses pass by about every half hour. From there, it's an hour to the nearest large town, and then two hours more to San Salvador.

No matter how often I come to El Salvador, the beauty of the country continually amazes me. There are volcanoes and mountain ranges, lakes, flowers, and shrubs growing wild as you drive the winding roads. Poinsettias bloom by the side of the road in the countryside, not just arriving in baskets for Christmas. There are 300 miles of beaches, including some of the best surfing spots in the world. For me, there is something majestic about sitting at a restaurant overlooking the ocean watching storms out at sea during the rainy season.

But the beauty can mask death and destruction that comes from the natural environment. Consider the five major natural hazards worldwide: hurricanes and related storms, tornadoes, earthquakes, tsunamis, and volcanoes.

Salvadorans face acute and immediate danger from three of these natural hazards—hurricanes, earthquakes, and volcanoes. Fortunately, tsunamis have not hit Central America in half a century and tornadoes there are rare. There are waterspouts (tornadoes at sea)—I have seen one—but no reports of tornadoes on land during the last 10 years.

In the past 15 years, El Salvador has endured 4 very destructive hurricanes or major storms. First came Hurricane Mitch in 1998, the deadliest North Atlantic hurricane since 1980. Sustained winds up to 180 miles per hour caused 240 deaths in El Salvador, and damaged more than 10,000 houses.

When Hurricane Stan hit El Salvador in October 2005, I was living there. The week that Hurricane Stan hovered over Central America, dropping inch after inch of rain, was one of the most depressing of my life. As all the schools and the universities in the country were closed that week, I stayed in my apartment, safe from flooding, working on my laptop on projects. All day long every day the rain came down, and every night I would turn on the news to hear of more deaths (82 in total) and of another 10,000 persons who had been driven out of their homes and into shelters. That weekend, when the rain had stopped, I went out with members of a Salvadoran non-profit to distribute supplies to one of the shelters set up temporarily in an elementary school to house those driven from their homes by the volcano and by flooding; up to 8 families were sleeping in each of the classrooms then. Students in at least 100 schools nationwide had their education interrupted until people could move back to their communities or into housing, and in some cases this took months.

The severe rain from Hurricane Ida in 2009 washed out bridges and roads, cutting off parts of the mountainous interior from the rest of the country and causing at least 184 deaths. In 2011 it was Tropical Depression 12-E. The term "tropical depression" sounds like a condition caused by too much sun and too many *mojitos*, but Tropical Depression 12-E, which lingered over El Salvador dumping rain for more than a week, caused massive destruction. While the death toll was only 34, thanks to an early warning system that has been put in place, the sustained rains severely hit the infrastructure—40% of the road network, 23 bridges, 500 schools, and hundreds of houses were destroyed. Many of the fall corn and *frijole* crops were lost during the rain. Over 270,000 producers, mostly small-scale farmers, suffered losses.

Earthquakes are also common in Central America, where the Cocos tectonic plate is being forced below the edge of two overriding plates: the North American to the northwest and the Caribbean to the southeast. Because of the movement and active interaction of these tectonic plates, hundreds of earthquakes of varying sizes are recorded every year throughout the region.

On January 13, 2001, a quake measuring 7.9 on the Richter scale struck El Salvador. At least 944 deaths resulted, 585 of these from landslides. More than 5,000 people were injured, over 100,000 houses were destroyed, and another 170,000 houses and more than 150,000 commercial buildings were damaged. There was damage in every department (state) in the country. In the weeks after the earthquake, there were more than 2,500 aftershocks, deeply unsettling the populace.

Then a month later, on February 13, 2001, a 6.6 magnitude earthquake struck 15 miles east of the capital, San Salvador. This quake caused 315 deaths, and almost 3,400 were injured; another 16,800 homes were damaged and 44,760 were destroyed—many of these buildings had been weakened in the first quake.

Both geologic and human factors contribute to the high number of deaths from landslides. Also, much of El Salvador is covered with volcanic soil, *tierra blanca* ash. This is silty sand, and its composition allows it to stand in near-vertical slopes. However, according to soil scientists, this soil is unstable in sustained rain and earthquakes, so earthquakes here cause landslides more often than they do elsewhere.

El Salvador, a country roughly the size of Massachusetts, is home to 22 volcanoes. Of these, 6 are considered active, which is to say that they could turn from peaceful to catastrophic at any time with devastating consequences (scientists have theorized that the Dark Ages in Europe were caused by an eruption of a volcano).

In El Salvador, there have been two eruptions of volcanoes in the last ten years. The most recent was in December 2013, when the San Miguel volcano, 90 miles east of the capital, sent a column of ash and debris 3 miles into the air and emitted high levels of hazardous sulfur dioxide. Over 3,000 people had to be evacuated after the eruption.

The Santa Ana volcano, located 27 miles west of San Salvador, erupted on October 1, 2005. There was no lava streaming over the top of the volcano, although there was an ash and gas plume that reached a height of over 8 miles, and several boulders the size of small cars were hurled from the volcano. One boulder hit and killed a farmer working in his fields. A torrent of boiling mud and water reaching 30 feet high streamed out of a vent in the side of the volcano, cutting a path 200 yards wide through the community of Palo Campana.

What comes from Mother Nature in El Salvador is both much more predictable in some ways and in others much less predictable than in the United States. I realized some time after getting to El Salvador in 2005 that the local TV news did not have weather reporting. There's no need for it on a daily basis. During the rainy season, from (more or less) April or May to November, it will rain at some point most days. During the dry season, which usually starts in late November and lasts 6 months, there will be no precipitation. The temperature does not fluctuate much all year long—a few degrees cooler in December and January than in other months.

Severe weather, on the other hand, can happen with little warning. With hurricanes, one can get a warning, but the strength and duration when the approaching storm hits landfall is very difficult to predict. With volcanoes, seismologists measure activity in active volcanoes, but prediction is inexact. In the case of the 2005 Santa Ana volcano, there had been news reports of increased activity in the volcano, but that had happened before without any eruptions.

The population density of El Salvador contributes to both its susceptibility to natural hazards and its ability to cope with them. As Simeon Tegel explains, only two percent of El Salvador's original forests remain, and the watersheds are unequal to the stresses caused by the increasingly frequent storms.

Building standards have been strengthened for commercial buildings, but people who are poor put up houses or shacks where they can find space, and these are very susceptible to collapse. In some cases, they are in the path of runoff or raging waters when there are hurricanes or other major storms.

The United Nations' *WorldRiskReport* 2012 ranked countries worldwide in terms of environmental risk based on 4 factors: exposure to natural hazards; susceptibility to harm depending on infrastructure, housing, and economic conditions; capacities to reduce negative consequences; and capacities for long-term adaptation to future natural events and climate change. El Salvador was ranked 10th—only 9 other countries are at greater risk. The challenges faced by El Salvador are shared in varying degrees by other Central American countries. In the *WorldRiskReport* cited above, Guatemala was ranked as having the 5th greatest risk, Costa Rica the 7th, and Nicaragua the 15th.

According to a 2011 report by CONARE, Central America is the most vulnerable tropical region to the impacts of climate change:

The beginning of the second decade of the 21st century may therefore be considered a particularly dangerous moment for the isthmus because the new threats greatly exceed the individual states' capacity to respond. Moreover, unlike thirty years ago, Central America must now confront this situation relatively alone, since the region has been losing its global importance (though not in all areas), both from the geopolitical standpoint and in terms of international cooperation.

How do all these factors affect youth in El Salvador? Because one often takes for granted the situation one has grown up in, youth rarely mention factors such as the size and density of the country and the natural beauty. In the surveys my co-researcher and I conducted in a rural area of northwestern El Salvador, the youth who were interviewed also rarely mentioned the splendor of the natural world. Salvadorans living in the United States, however, will talk about and reminisce about the beauty of the country.

Similarly, except for those youth who live in areas susceptible to flooding, the environmental precariousness—especially from earthquakes and volcanoes—does not seem to be a major concern. The impact of natural disasters was not mentioned as a significant problem area in the two most recent surveys of youth. For youth, it seems that the preoccupation with personal safety and finding a place in the economy tend to crowd out other issues.

3

Past to Present

The Roman philosopher and politician Cicero said: "To remain ignorant of things that happened before you were born is to remain a child." There is a tendency to assume that things in a country have always been the way they are now. In El Salvador, the country that young people are growing up in was shaped not only by the civil war decades earlier but also by events over the past almost five centuries.

Like much of Latin America, the boundaries and borders of El Salvador bear the imprint of the Spanish conquest. Before the Spanish arrived in the 16th century, in the eastern part of what is now El Salvador there lived the Lenca, related to the Maya in Guatemala. In the western part were the Pipil, related to the Aztecs in Mexico, who had migrated there around 1000 A.D. These groups established city states; the largest of these, Cuscatlan, had a population of up to 10,000.

The Spanish conquest and colonization of El Salvador began with the arrival of an expedition from Guatemala in 1524 led by the *conquistador* Pedro de Alvarado. Around the same time, another group of Spaniards from the earlier conquest of Panama entered the territory of what is now El Salvador from Nicaragua. The native *Indios* resisted fiercely, but the combination of superior weapons and the impact of smallpox and other diseases for which they had no immunity prevailed. By 1540, the Spaniards controlled all of what is now El Salvador, and it became a province of Guatemala. Controlling the country involved seizing and then parceling out the large fertile tracts of lands to individual Spaniards. For the Spanish government with its Central American headquarters in Guatemala, there was wealth to be gained through exports. In the 1500s, it was cocoa. By the 1700s the rich blue dye indigo had become popular in Europe. The native population was forced to work on large holdings to cultivate indigo.

By the late 1700s, the landowning elite was chafing under the rules and restrictions from the Spanish rulers in Guatemala, which were generally designed to aid Guatemalan merchants. Following the proclamation of Mexican independence in 1821, El Salvador endorsed Guatemala's declaration of independence from Spain and became a part of the Federal Republic of Central America. With the collapse of this in 1840, El Salvador became independent in 1841.

For the next 30 years, there were ongoing conflicts between Guatemala and El Salvador related to Salvadoran independence from Guatemala. The Guatemalan ruler, Raúl Carrera, on multiple occasions installed military leaders or other supporters as El Salvador's president.

From the 1870s to the late 1920s, governmental policies were to support through the growth of infrastructure and laws the exportation of coffee without interfering with the free operation of market forces. By 1890, coffee counted for more than 80% of El Salvador's exports. An oligarchy—an elite group of influential landowners referred to as the Fourteen Families—constituted the real power in the country. Governmental policies included the development of railroad lines to the ports, the elimination of communal landholdings so that land would no longer be used for subsistence farming, and laws against vagrancy. The loss of the common lands and the laws against vagrancy meant that *campesinos*, the rural poor, were forced to work on the coffee *fincas* (plantations) for low wages.

In the 1927 presidential election, a reformer named Pio Romero Bosque was elected, and he pledged to work for a new public culture based on mutual respect and shared responsibilities for all classes in Salvadoran society. The collapse of the Salvadoran (and world) economy in the Great Depression and the opposition of the landowning elite stymied his reforms. In 1931, he was followed as president by another reformer, Arturo Araujo, who was overthrown in a military coup nine months later. General Maximiliano Hernández Martinez then declared himself president. Hernández Martinez reacted to a 2-day revolt by farmworkers in 1932 by crushing the rebellion and executing between 10,000 and 40,000 persons suspected of being involved. Today, this event is referred to by Salvadorans as *La Matanza* (the slaughter).

The large landowners, observing both the dangers of insurgency and the value of a military dictatorship, lent their support to the military for the next 40+ years. Military dictatorships and elections in which military officers gained the presidency through intimidation and voter fraud continued until 1979.

By the 1970s, the rule of military leaders supported by the oligarchy was challenged. A portion of the discontent came from the increased land concentration in the country. Going back to the late 1800s, a quarter of the cultivable land in the country had been communal property—anyone in a village could graze their cattle or plant corn there. This land was privatized to increase the size of coffee fincas and other plantations. The concentration of land and wealth which started in the 19th century continued in the 20th century and accelerated in the 1960s. In a country that was very rural at the time, 19.8% of the population did not own land in 1961; by 1971, that figure had increased to 41.1%. In 1970, the poorest fifth of the population earned only 3.7% of the national income, and the richest fifth earned 50.8%. By 1980, the country had become even more unequal, with the richest 20% earning 66% of the national income and the poorest 20% earning just 2%.

For the dispossessed, there now seemed to be an alternative, the socialist model announced from Cuba every night through the broadcasts of Radio Havana. I remember walking through a squatter community one night in 1972 and a resident asking me if it was true that Cuba had the highest literacy rate in the Americas (it was).

The labor unions, peasant groups, and other leftist organizations carried out strikes, demonstrations, and parades in the 1970s, and they were joined by a new ally, Catholic priests. In the 1970s, Catholicism was by far the predominant church in the country. From the Second Vatican Council in 1962 called by Pope John XXIII and a Latin America bishops' conference in 1968, there arose a strong emphasis on social justice and reform. As Leonardo and Clodovis Boff, prominent liberation theologians, explain, it was felt that the Bible should be read and experienced from the perspective of the poor. On how one is to be a Christian in a world of destitution and injustice, Boff and Boff say, "there can be only one answer: we can be followers of Jesus and true Christians only by making common cause with the poor and working out the gospel of liberation."

Many Salvadoran priests embraced liberation theology, and activist clergy brought this new social reading of Christ's life and the Scriptures to their preaching and work. This, along with the training of catechists and lay personnel, transformed the consciousness of a large part of the rural population. When these *campesinos* began to organize, advocate for better wages and working conditions, and gain access to credit, they were met by violent repression. From this repression came the genesis of revolution.

While liberation theology was applying a critical Christian analysis to issues of the poor, at the same time an educational approach focused on political and economic injustice was developing. In Brazil, Paolo Freire was developing an approach for teaching illiterate and semi-literate campesinos to read and to critically analyze their life situations. In his most famous work, *Pedagogy of the Oppressed*, Freire maintained that education is never neutral. Through education, people can understand their social, political, and economic context and begin to transform their world. In early-1970s El Salvador, organizers, leftists, and members of revolutionary groups began to work with the poor in rural areas and low-income San Salvador communities using Freire's framework of *concientización*. (This is usually translated as "consciousness raising," but I think that the phrase "becoming aware" hits closest to its meaning.)

I arrived in El Salvador in 1970 during this time of clerical and popular discontent and unrest. When I got to El Salvador in 1970, I was told by many Salvadorans that they had a military dictatorship disguised as a democracy. The ruling party, the National Conciliation Party (PCN), had been in power since 1960. Backed by the military and with policies benefiting the rich, the PCN was a patronage organization that dispensed favors to party loyalists. In 1972, Napoleon Duarte, the former mayor of San Salvador, ran for the presidency as the Christian Democratic Party candidate, with a number of small parties and leftist organizations supporting his candidacy. Elections were held on Sunday, February 12, and the next day the Central Election Board in San Salvador issued a statement that unofficial counts had Duarte winning by at least 6,000 votes. There was then a news blackout for three days, and Friday afternoon we heard that the official count, with great differences from the original tallies in several cities, had the PCN candidate winning the election. After this election, which everyone I knew believed was fraudulent, you could feel the tension in the air. In the communities in which I worked, neighborhood residents stated that you had to be careful about what you said, because there were government informers everywhere. When I asked one diplomat I knew in the U.S. Embassy about informers, he told me that there were perhaps 10,000—and very few people vetting or analyzing the information. Someone who did not like you could say that you were a Communist, and you might get "disappeared." When I left El Salvador to return to the United States later in 1972, I could literally feel the weight leave my shoulders as the plane got into the air.

During the next seven years the unrest increased. The 1974 election results had no credibility—the government announced that its party, the PCN, had won, but they did not list vote totals. Mass popular organizations continued with strikes and protests. Response and repression came not only from the government but also from the Democratic Nationalist Organization (ORDEN). ORDEN was a paramilitary network and rural vigilante force that was operating death squads. In the countryside there were reports in the 1970s of ORDEN and National Guard forces hacking civilian opponents of the government to death with machetes. At times the bodies would be left on the side of a road as a warning to others.

In the city of San Salvador, protests continued, and in 1975 police fired on a crowd protesting the government's spending a million dollars to hold the Miss Universe contest in El Salvador. The police killed at least twelve and wounded many others. During this time period, leftist groups carried out kidnappings of members of rich families—some of the time the kidnappings ended in ransom paid, sometimes the kidnapped person was killed.

Most people consider the start of the war to be 1979, and it did not officially end until the signing of the Peace Accords 12 years later. From my point of view, there were four major players and one smaller player in the civil war, and their priorities, actions, and inactions contributed to the conflict lasting as long as it did.

First, there were the landowners—those who controlled (and still control) much of the land, manufacturing, and large commercial enterprises. According to Hugh Byrne in *El Salvador's Civil War*, their power in the country was magnified by the fact that there were no other large competing bases of power. Also, unlike other Latin American countries, the military was not involved in economic enterprise, so armed forces officers were not competitors to wealthy landowners.

The second group of major players were the Armed Forces of El Salvador. They traditionally allied with the landowners, and were for the most part conservative (more progressive army officers were moved aside in the 1970s). As the conflict escalated, the Armed Forces grew from 17,000 in 1980 to 56,000 in 1987, almost entirely due to United States military aid.

Aligned with the government and allegedly directed by Army officers were right-wing death squads, funded in large part by rich Salvadorans living in Miami or Europe. The death squads targeted those on the left or suspected to be on the left. By late 1979, estimates of those murdered reached 800 every month. As Mark Danner writes:

> *As the repression went on, month after month, it became less and less discriminating. William Stanley, a professor of political science at the University of New Mexico told me: "By the end, the killing basically outran the intelligence capability of the Armed forces and the security services, and they began killing according to very crude profiles. I remember, for example, hearing that a big pile of corpses was discovered, and almost all of them turned out be young women wearing jeans and tennis shoes. Apparently, one of the intelligence people had decided that this 'profile'—you know, young women who dressed in that way—made it easy to separate out 'leftists' and so that became one of the profiles that they used to round up so-called subversives."*

The assassinations continued with the murder of the archbishop of San Salvador, Oscar Romero, on March 24, 1980. Romero had been selected as archbishop because he was a moderate who had not been involved in social issues. However, the assassination of a priest who was his friend and the increasing frequency and brutality of the violence moved him to speak out. His weekly homilies on the radio were widely listened to, and in these he relayed statistics on murders carried out by the government-supported death squads and government troops. The day after delivering a homily in which he called on soldiers to refuse to carry out orders that he characterized as immoral, he was assassinated while conducting Mass.

According to testimony by ex-U.S. ambassador Robert White, there was sufficient evidence to convict former Major Roberto D'Aubisson of planning and ordering Archbishop Romero's assassination. D'Aubisson, who organized death squads that carried out kidnappings, torture, and killings to intimidate opponents of the elite, later formed the ARENA political party.

When 250,000 mourners gathered for the funeral of Romero, presumed government snipers attacked the crowd, killing 42 and wounding over 200. After this, insurgent action against the government increased.

A third major player in the civil war was the "left." This broad term encompassed everyone from progressive intellectuals and priests and others interested in social reform to Communist activists and the guerrilla groups that had taken up arms in different parts of the country. In 1980, the differing guerrilla groups joined with leftist parties to form the *Frente Farabundo Marti para la Liberación Nacional* (Farabundo Marti National Liberation Front) or the FMLN. Throughout the war these armed groups operated in different parts of the country and by the latter parts of the war they were coordinating their strategies and attacks.

Along with the large landowners, the military, and the left, the fourth major player was the United States. Its actions were influenced by other global forces at play that made this more than an internal conflict in a small Central American country. In the late 1970s, the Cold War between the United States and Russia that had started after World War II continued, with both sides intent on gaining influence in all parts of the world. The image of countries as dominos—if one country "falls to Communism," the neighbor will then fall, and so on—was still popular.

In July 1979, a revolutionary force named the Sandinistas took power in Nicaragua. From then on, starting with the presidency of Jimmy Carter and intensifying during the presidency of Ronald Reagan, the struggle in El Salvador was seen primarily not as a civil war but as part of the larger struggle against the Soviet Union and its allies. When Jimmy Carter was president, his administration was pressuring the Salvadoran government on human rights and land reform that would limit the holdings and influence of the elite. When Reagan became president in 1980, the United States' interest then narrowed to stopping the "Communist menace." In May 1984, President Reagan stated: "San Salvador is closer to Houston, Texas, than Houston is to Washington, DC. Central America is America. It's at our doorstep, and it's become the stage for a bold attempt by the Soviet Union, Cuba, and Nicaragua, to install Communism by force throughout the hemisphere." Without the perceived threat of Soviet dominance in the hemisphere, there would not have been the massive support from the United States, and without that support the civil war would have ended sooner and perhaps differently.

The United States gave the Salvadoran government between $4.2 billion and $6 billion from 1980 to 1992 for both economic and military assistance. The U.S. public was told that American servicemen were in El Salvador as military advisors and were not involved in the fighting. Years later, U.S. Army veterans sought recognition for their combat service in El Salvador. I was talking at a charity golf outing a few years ago with someone about my age, and I happened to mention my ongoing research. "El Salvador?" he replied, "I flew helicopters there during the war."

I had stated that there were four major players and one minor player, and there was also the minor (but not unimportant) support that the rebel groups received from Cuba, Nicaragua, and the Soviet Union. Arms, especially Russian-made AK-47s no longer being used in Vietnam, entered from Nicaragua or indirectly from Honduras. In the last years of the war, surface-to-air missiles were used to bring down Armed Forces helicopters; this negated the advantage in the air that the Armed forces previously held.

Although unlike that of the key players mentioned above, the role of the Salvadoran populace was critical, especially the large majority that did not actively support either side. Their actions (and inaction) played a large part in the war ending how and when it did.

Why did the war last for over a decade? One reason is that while negotiations between the government and the FMLN were held from time to time, neither side wanted to make serious concessions. The elite backing the military and the U.S. were both sure that they could win, as was the FMLN.

Another reason was that the Armed Forces were far from effective. Much of the military was stationary, guarding fixed resources like power plants and large government buildings, especially as the guerrillas had been successful in disrupting power supplies and attacking remote army outposts. Commanders would often engage in sweeps with thousands of troops in rebel areas, moving slowly with heavy equipment; the rebels would often slip away, only to return after the government troops left. It was said that senior officers were more interested in inflating the size of their battalions—and collecting the pay of nonexistent soldiers—than in defeating the insurgents. While the size and experience of the troops of the Armed Forces increased in the latter years of the war, changes in tactics by the guerrillas took their toll—especially with the use of landmines and, later, ground-to-air missiles.

The rebel forces engaged in a campaign of economic sabotage throughout the war that was effective. Their attacks on the economy—through destruction of dams, power stations, export crops and their processing plants, and telephone and electrical systems—crippled the economy in many parts of the country, diminishing tax revenue. It was only through the support of the U.S. government that the shortfall between government revenues and expenses was met and the war effort sustained.

The 1982 elections were favorable for legislators supporting the government, and a presidential candidate backed by the government and the United States was elected in 1984. In actuality, support for the government never substantially increased. In part, this was because the elite blocked land reform measures that had been a priority of the U.S. government. Government plans to develop citizens' patrols and civic organizations in areas where rebels had influence never materialized, largely because of intimidation by the FMLN. Overall, there was not much support for an ineffective government that did not seem to have the people's well-being as a top priority.

In late 1989, a series of events contributed to an overall consensus that the war had to end. On November 9, the Berlin Wall fell, and after that, U.S. President George Herbert Walker Bush was not in favor of continuing major financial support to the Salvadoran government. The United States and Russia were no longer waging war with each other through surrogate states, and the era of open conflict in Latin America had ended.

Two days after the Berlin Wall fell, the FMLN launched an offensive in the capital city of San Salvador. Two thousand guerrillas entered the city, holding some neighborhoods for several days until air strikes forced them to leave. They attacked wealthy neighborhoods and provoked a military response that killed 1,000 civilians. While the offensive did not trigger the popular insurrection that the FMLN had desired, it did demonstrate that the guerrillas were still a potent fighting force.

Another event that increased pressure to end the war occurred on November 16, 1989. Six Jesuit priests at the Catholic University, along with their housekeeper and her daughter, were pulled from their beds and shot—a murder ordered by senior military officials. This action and the government cover-up outraged the world and led to a concerted outcry in the U.S. to end military aid to the Salvadoran government.

By 1990, both sides had realized that neither could prevail in this civil war. Separately, each side approached the United Nations for help in negotiating a settlement. The United Nations' sponsored talks led to the signing of the Peace Accords on January 16, 1992, ending 12 years of civil war.

The Peace Accords contained structural changes that affected the combatants in the war. There was a major reduction in the size of the country's armed forces, and the feared state-run police force, the *Guardia Nacional,* was disbanded. The various guerrilla groups put down their arms and disbanded as fighting units; the FMLN became a political party. A new police force was created, with a third from the Army, a third from the guerrillas, and a third from civilians.

Opening up the political process and ending the military's dominant role in the county were significant enough that UN mediator Alvaro de Soto described the Peace Accords as a "negotiated revolution." However, as anthropologist Leigh Binford remarked, the accords "did not initiate an era of greater social and economic justice." The Accords did not include land reform or other provisions that would benefit the 400,000 people, mostly *campesinos*, who had lost their homes in the conflict.

Also, half a million Salvadorans left during the war, mostly emigrating to the United States. These included a large number of young men, who left because both the armed forces and the guerrillas were forcibly drafting youth 16 years of age and younger. I have met a number of Salvadoran men in the United States, now in their early 50s, whose stories are remarkably similar. They went north either out of fear of having to be combatants or because they served with the armed forces or the rebels and then left for the U.S.

In March 1993, the UN-appointed Commission on the Truth for El Salvador published *From Madness to Hope: The 12-Year War in El Salvador*. This report attributed the overwhelming majority of the human rights abuses to the Salvadoran Armed Forces and the death squads linked to the Salvadoran Armed Forces, as well as the assassination of Archbishop Oscar Romero and the deaths of six Jesuit priests. The killing of mayors and members of the government as well as kidnappings, bombings, and extra-judicial killings were attributed to the guerrilla militias.

Five days after the Commission's report was released, the Salvadoran legislature, controlled by conservatives, approved an amnesty law covering all violent events of the war. The amnesty law is still in effect. With the amnesty, no members of the Armed Forces, ORDEN, or guerrillas/FMLN have been charged and tried for war crimes.

The conservative party ARENA, which had gained the presidency in the elections of 1989, intensified the neoliberal economic policies that had been initiated in previous years. Neoliberal policies, which were promoted by the World Bank and the United States, included the shrinking of the size of the government, reduction of trade barriers, the privatization of state companies, loosening of regulations, and encouragement of foreign and domestic investment.

In 1995 and 1996, there were massive public layoffs. The Salvadoran economy, which had been strong in the early years of the 1990s, slowed down. At the same time, there was a need for workers in the booming United States economy, and the border between Mexico and the U.S. was far easier to cross then. A half-million Salvadorans had gone to the U.S. during the civil war, and an increasing number of Salvadorans left in the mid and late 1990s to seek work and to reunite with family members in the United States. In El Salvador, there was an increase in violence during this time. In 1995, there were 7,877 homicides—138.9 murders per 100,000. This was the highest homicide rate in Latin America, second in the world. The problems with violence, theft, robbery, sexual assaults, and gangs were generally seen by commentators as the problem. The commentators failed to fully acknowledge the connections between the violence and the country's issues with poverty, lack of opportunity, and inequality.

ARENA had won the presidency in 1994 and 1999. By 2004, dissatisfaction with the state of the economy and the government's handling of crime and violence gave early indications that the opposition, the FMLN, would win. Two years earlier, the FMLN had almost won a majority in the national legislature and had elected a record number of mayors. However, many saw the FMLN candidate Schafik Handal, one of the guerrilla commanders in the civil war, as a Marxist ideologue. This impression of Handal was reinforced weeks before the election when Handal praised Fidel Castro's jailing of political prisoners in Cuba. In the run-up to the election, ARENA played on the fears of the Salvadoran populace, which had become increasingly dependent on remittances sent back from family members working in the U.S.

The ARENA candidate, Antonio (Tony) Saca, based his campaign on how an FMLN win could affect relations with the U.S. This television spot ran repeatedly in the days before the election, showing a middle-class Salvadoran couple receiving a phone call from their son, who is in Los Angeles working on a temporary work visa:

"Mom, I wanted to let you know that I'm scared," the young man says.

"Why?" his mother asks.

"Because if Schafik becomes president of El Salvador, I may be deported," her son answers, *"and you won't be able to receive the remittances that I'm sending you."*

Saca won the election with 57% of the vote.

In 2009, the FMLN chose as its candidate Mauricio Funes, a television journalist who had come to prominence in 1984 with his incisive comments on wartime El Salvador. Unlike other FMLN presidential candidates, Funes did not fit the "revolutionary turned politician" mold. He did not even become a member of the FMLN until he declared for the presidency. Funes promised "safe change," patterning himself after Brazil's center-leftist president Luiz Inácio Lula da Silva. The ARENA candidate, Rodrigo Avila, the former director of the National Civilian Police, ran an uninspiring campaign. The slow pace of economic growth and the rising problem with violence during the presidency of Tony Saca did not help Avila's campaign.

Funes won the election with 51.3% of the votes. During his administration, he was often at odds with his party, at times vetoing FMLN-supported proposals. Proposals enacted during Funes' term broadened the social safety net through income transfers, especially to the poorest elderly, and increased social and health services. They provided free uniforms, shoes, and school supplies to poor children attending public schools. Some tax reforms were enacted, but not to the degree desired by the FMLN.

Funes maintained a strong relationship with the United States during his presidency. While he re-established diplomatic ties with Cuba during the first days of his presidency, he supported the Obama administration on several initiatives and did not withdraw the small number of Salvadoran troops stationed in Afghanistan as part of the United States-led coalition. Partly because of this, the U.S. government renewed temporary work permits (TPS) for almost 300,000 Salvadorans working in the United States and provided expanded aid for development projects.

In 2014, in addition to the FMLN and ARENA, there was a third party contesting for the 5-year presidency. Tony Saca, the ARENA candidate who had won the presidency in 2004, split from ARENA and ran again under the auspices of the UNIDAD coalition. The FMLN nominated Salvador Sanchez Cerén, vice-president to Funes and a guerrilla commander in the civil war. ARENA nominated Norman Quijano, the mayor of San Salvador.

Sanchez Cerén almost won the presidency outright in the primary, getting 48.92% of the popular vote; 50% plus one vote is needed to avoid a runoff. Quijano had 38.95% of the vote, and Saca only 11.44%. While it appeared that Sanchez Cerén would win easily, ARENA's more effective "get out the vote" effort and a media campaign linking the FMLN with riots and economic scarcity in Venezuela at the time of the election narrowed the race. Salvador Cerén won the presidency, but with less than a 7,000-vote margin.

While the ARENA party claimed fraud after the elections, the Organization of American States, the U.S. State Department, and other international observers described the process as orderly, transparent, and clean. One of the pillars of a democratic society, the Supreme Electoral Tribunal (TSE), functioned very well in the 2014 election.

How do the events of the past centuries, the civil war, and the two decades since the signing of the Peace Accords affect young Salvadorans coming of age? The polarization of the country along political and economic lines is not unique to El Salvador. However, that the two major political parties today formed from the opposing sides in the civil war personalizes politics for many people in a way that I can only begin to comprehend. If your relatives were tortured or "disappeared" by death squads under the command of Roberto D'Aubisson, the founder of ARENA, then you could have a visceral reaction against that party. If you had an uncle who was kidnapped by the guerrillas, then the FMLN could always be linked in your mind with terrorism.

Also, the war was not that long ago, and many adults were combatants then. A librarian I know was a soldier in the Armed Forces. After meeting with a researcher at a small institute that worked on community issues, my co-researcher Virginia Quintana told me: "She was a *subcomandante*." I could picture the middle-aged woman we had been talking to as she looked decades earlier, an AK-47 slung across her shoulder. As the American novelist William Faulkner once said, "The past is never dead. It's not even past."

STORIES

4

Individual Stories

For the most part, these stories come from interviews that I have conducted in El Salvador over the past several years, and I wanted to let the stories stand for themselves rather than just including snippets in chapters to illustrate various points. Most of the stories come from Salvadorans who have come of age in the last decade—the youngest in their early 20s, the oldest now a decade older. The two exceptions to this are my own story of my involvement in El Salvador, and Daniel's story, as told by Danny Burridge.

Jim Winship

I am including my story in this section although I am no longer a youth, clearly not Salvadoran. Including the story of my experiences in El Salvador may help the reader understand the lens through which I view the country. Also, in the process of writing this book, going back through letters and memories of my Peace Corps years right out of college, I have become aware of how important El Salvador was in my own coming of age.

In the spring of 1970, months before graduating from college, I received an invitation from the Peace Corps to spend two years serving in the country of El Salvador. In those days before Google, I went to an encyclopedia to find out where exactly El Salvador was located. I accepted the invitation.

Later that summer, three weeks into the in-country training in El Salvador, I was becoming friends with Marc, a Volunteer who had been there a year. Marc worked in the program where I would serve—community organizing with the Department of Community Action in the Mayor's Office of San Salvador.

Marc lived in a room in a community center in the largest blighted area in the city, La Chacra, where he worked. He invited me one day to come to La Chacra and we walked down the muddy street that led into the neighborhood. I remember that first impression as if it just happened. Tiny houses, packed close together, made of wood and cardboard, dirt floors, tin roofs. Pigs and chickens walking in the streets, along with half-naked children, some of them with protruded bellies, a sure sign of malnutrition. So many sights, so many sounds. I'm having trouble putting one foot in front of another, not stopping to stare, paralyzed. I keep saying to myself, as if as a mantra, over and over again, "it's almost this bad in the hollers of Kentucky, I've seen worse in Morocco...it's almost this bad in the hollers of Kentucky, I've seen worse in Morocco...." I feel like I am putting on mental blinders to keep from being overwhelmed.

I don't remember anything else about that visit. The next day, three Volunteers, who would also be working in the Department of Community Action, asked if I wanted to join them in renting a house in a working class section of San Salvador. The house was nothing fancy, but with real floors and running water and electricity.

After thinking about it, I asked Marc if he could find me a family in La Chacra who could rent me a room. He did, and I decided to live in a room of Manuel Antonio España's family's house. I had realized that the chasm between the world I was used to and the life in those communities was so great that the only way I would be effective was to live there. Otherwise, I'd go to work in the morning, and come home to an English-speaking house with other Volunteers in the evening, and could spend the two years without more than starting to understand the people I was working with— the people I was supposed to be helping.

It was inconvenient to not have indoor plumbing and running water, but what I got in return was the experience of living with a family, in a house full of young children, cats, and dogs. Yes, I went to too many wakes of kids who died too young. But I also smiled at the budding soccer stars kicking balls or cans or whatever they could find. I walked the streets on New Year's Eve, with the smell of cordite from revolvers fired in the air and the sounds of music playing everywhere. I would walk down to Jorge's house. One of the community leaders, a house painter, joked that we would go into business together. As I was a foot and a half taller than he, he would paint the bottom part of a wall, and I the top. The experience there of la *vida cotidiana,* the day-to-day life, both enriched my under-standing of the communities in which I worked and also served as a refuge from work, a place to come to and play with young children, or talk about nothing more consequential than the weather.

I was working both in communities where people owned small (25-yard by 50-yard) plots of land, with hand-built houses, and in communities where the people were squatting. The work for the most part involved community projects. In one community, we turned a dirt road into one that was essentially cobble-stoned, so that the road would be passable in the rainy season. In another community, I helped the elected group of leaders, the *directiva,* ac-quire the materials to build a community center.

There were also aspects of the job that were controversial. I was denounced on a radio call-in show for my work in a different com-munity, where residents squatted as the title of the land had been tied up and fought over in courts for more than a decade. Some residents in that community also participated in the first land invasion in Central America, in which over 300 people descended on and occupied a vacant piece of land one evening.

It was a heady job for a 22-year-old just out of college. I was working in a second language in a position that was important but had little structure, and it was hard to tell how well I was doing.

I learned much from the community residents with whom I worked, few of whom had more than a 3rd-grade education. I remember vividly one night, as one of those groups was struggling for consensus, realizing that there were layers on top of layers of meaning in the words that were spoken. Now, in the planning groups and committees and boards on which I serve, I endeavor to listen for the hidden concerns and agendas.

I had the opportunity to cross lines of class and power. I wrote this in a letter in 1971:

> *I believe that I know this country more deeply than I know the United States, at least more aspects of it. Yesterday I went to the Mayor's Office, talked with my co-workers (lower middle class). After meeting with engineers about bridge construction in one of the communities where I worked, I returned to where I lived. I ran into several of the men there that I had gotten to know, and we talked and joked about politics and revolution. In the afternoon I went to a movie with a Peace Corps Volunteer who had come in from the countryside, then went to a community to help prepare for a visit by the Mayor that evening. After the meeting, the man who had sold the lots in the community, a rich young lawyer, invited the Mayor, the Assistant Director of Acción Communitaria, and myself to his house. We drank and talked until two in the morning. Not a typical day, but there aren't typical days.*

After I left El Salvador in 1972, I did not get back until 2005, more than 30 years later. There were reasons for the long delay in returning—the civil war, the preoccupation with our raising a family, and work. In the early 2000s I found myself thinking more and more about El Salvador.

Overall, my Peace Corps experience had been powerful, and I

did not want to just get off the plane in San Salvador as a tourist. Whenever I thought about going back, it was difficult to imagine what it would be like to just get a ticket and fly down. I had lost touch with all the people I had known, Salvadorans and *gringos* alike.

Throughout these years, I had been periodically checking for Fulbright Scholars opportunities in El Salvador. The Fulbright Scholars Program, a part of the federal State Department, sends around 1,100 American scholars and professionals each year to approximately 125 countries, where they lecture and/or conduct research in a large number of academic and professional fields. In 2004, I saw that one of the requested areas for Fulbright Scholars in El Salvador was a position to teach social work. I showed it to my wife, and her response was, "they wrote that for you." Well, not really, but I certainly fit the qualifications. The university where I have taught social work for decades, the University of Wisconsin-Whitewater, was kind enough to give me support and a leave if I received the Fulbright Award.

I did receive it, and spent 6 months in 2005 at the Universidad Panamericana de El Salvador. I did some teaching and made a documentary called *Difficult Dreams* about youth there. I also trained (with the help of Suzanne Kent, an anthropology doctoral student on a Fulbright) a group of students in qualitative research, and with them I conducted my first study on youth and migration. The result, *Una Familia, Dos Paises (One Family, Two Countries: Understanding the Impact on Youth When Their Parent(s) Emigrate to the United States)* was the first of my publications with Virginia Quintana, a researcher at the Universidad Panamericana. Together, we have conducted seven studies—five on youth and migration. A number of these have been published in Spanish.

Since 2005, I have been back to El Salvador 14 times. I have been able to move across different "worlds" there, as I did in my Peace Corps years. My friend Eva calls this "Gringo Power," meaning that I have been able to get access to high-ranking officials unavailable to others. I think that this comes from the combination of being an American, knowing the language, and having a Ph.D. I have been able to meet with six Cabinet Ministers in recent years. My research has taken me to poor rural communities and central city neighborhoods. Occasionally, I have spent time with Salvadorans from families of wealth and power, swimming at a private beach and drinking in a bar built into a swimming pool with a member of one of El Salvador's Fourteen Families.

But I spend far more time in El Salvador with people whose lives are far from wealth and power. At the Universidad Panamericana, eating lunch with the office staff, I have gotten to know these young, female high-school graduates whom one would describe as lower-middle class. Several of their accounts of what it is like to live in areas where gangs are very present inform my chapter on violence.

As should be clear from this writing, I have an affinity for the country and people of El Salvador. I drew laughs in a professional conference where we had been discussing the influence of the "*sueño Americano*" (American dream) on migration when I stated (only somewhat jokingly) that I was seeking the "*sueño Salvadoreño.*"

Douglas

I met Douglas in 2005. As a Fulbright Scholar at the Universidad Panamericana, I offered several workshops on program evaluation that were open to those working in non-profit organizations, and sent the announcement out through various groups. Signing up for the workshop was one of the staff members at the Maria Madre de los Pobres Parish located at the edge of the area known as La Chacra.

I was excited when I saw that there was someone from the parish, as I was interested in getting to know someone from La Chacra. I had lived there as a Peace Corps Volunteer and had wanted to return when I came back to the country, but was told that it was too dangerous—a dividing line between the two major gangs ran through the area, which included five separate neighborhoods.

I did talk to the nurse who came from the clinic attached to the parish, and was able to tour the area. I also met Douglas Jimenez, who came to the workshop as he wanted to talk about studying in the United States. I put him in touch with the programs that the U.S. Embassy had for Salvadorans, and he agreed to be interviewed for the documentary I made, Difficult Dreams.

Douglas was tall for a Salvadoran—and intense. In 2005, he was more interested in talking about the youth in the area than he was in talking about himself.

This area—there are 10 neighborhoods here—it is the largest concentration of poor people in El Salvador. And in this parish, there is a health clinic, with support from a number of countries. And with scholarships from Spain and the United States, 115 students are on scholarships, high school and college. The scholarships pay half the cost of the tuition.

There is also help with homework at the parish. For 4 years I was in charge of this program. Because of that, I had the chance to go to Western Michigan University and talk with youth there— as a representative of the parish. I got a chance to see how the educational system works there. I also got to meet delegations from other countries—from Europe, South Africa, the United States and Canada—and showed them around the area.

And the church, it has helped my spiritual life. I see the needs of the people well, what they need, and how to be more conscious and how to help others. Other than that—the church has helped me to broaden my horizons, to realize that money is not everything. A philosophy professor (*at the Universidad Centroamericana José Simeón Cañas—the UCA*) taught me that the most important thing in life is not the material things but your mind.

But this area, it has changed. Ten years ago, children were playing outside until 8:00 or 9:00 p.m. Now, there is no one out at that time. It's like a curfew that the gangs have imposed.

I have never felt such anxiety and fear as I do now. It's hard. You're walking around, you don't know whether to shake hands, greet someone. They know that you are involved with the parish—you might be talking to the police.

It's hard, and the youth here, to make money, to help their families, 85% of them think about going to the United States. About a fifth of those leave, but only maybe quarter of those make it. I know some who have made it to the United States. Those that are turned back, many try again, and they are always thinking of trying again.

It's a problem. This includes classmates at the university, who think about leaving—and staying there. From my point of view, if we who have the privilege of getting an education when others do not, including professionals, engineers, if we do not return, we will always be a country dependent on others, not sustaining itself.

In 2011, when I met Danny Burridge, whose account is in this section, I mentioned that I had interviewed Douglas for the documentary. "Oh, I know Douglas," he said, and gave me Douglas' cell phone number. We corresponded, and the following year Douglas drove to the apartment where I was staying in San Salvador for an interview.

It had been seven years since I saw him, and when I look at the pictures from the two time periods I see the difference between an earnest youth and a confident young man. In 2005 he had been a year away from college graduation. Danny had told me that Douglas had a good job, so I asked him to tell me the story of how he got to where he is now.

I dropped out of school before starting high school. I was 14. So I worked in construction for a year, and I saw that it was necessary to get that education. It was hard work, and I knew I wanted to go back to school. When my sister (*who later became a lawyer*) told me about the possibility of a scholarship, well, I applied, and got it. It was from St. Thomas More parish in the United States, in Kalamazoo, Michigan. The scholarship not only paid for my high school expenses but opened my eyes to possibilities, and to the idea that there were people outside El Salvador who wanted to help us.

I was fortunate to get the scholarship, because my parents could not help me with my education. My parents both work in the informal sector, as vendors. In the public market they sell underwear and socks. My dad was drinking a lot those days, and my mom would get up early to go to work and get home late.

In high school, I applied to the UCA, was accepted, and also got a scholarship there. 1999–2006. Between those two scholarships, they paid for 100% of my expenses.

I studied accounting, but I also learned a lot of things from the Jesuits. They showed me about humanity, and about how when you get an education, you have to help your brothers and sisters, to be a human, to be a good person.

So I needed a job, and shortly after graduation I got hired as a tax auditor. In El Salvador, many of the jobs you get because you know someone, through pull. But for mine, I took tests—a psychological test, math tests, several accounting tests. Maybe for higher-level positions it is who you know, your uncle or brother-in-law, but not for my position. I like the job. Doesn't pay too well (*but well enough for Douglas to have a car*), and sometimes the work is difficult. We are getting people to pay their taxes, and you know, people don't want to pay their taxes.

I am married now, for two years (*he showed me pictures of his wife and his one-year-old son, Gandhi*). I named him Gandhi, because I read a lot about him—you know, he was a very unique person.

I still live in La Chacra. I don't want to leave. Believe me, I never think about leaving our neighborhood. I am happy there. That is where I grew up. A lot of people don't have that impression. The people here—they are humans. There is life here.

Thelma

My co-researcher and I had first met Thelma when we conduct-ed focus groups with high schools in 2008. She was interviewed in our follow-up study on young women who had graduated from high school in 2010, and this is taken from her interview. To find out about her plans since then, my co-researcher Virginia Quintana interviewed her again briefly in 2014.

I was born and have grown up here in Hacienda Vieja. My fam-ily is unusual because my father lives and works here. He is a Health Promoter who goes to all the small communities and teaches peo-ple about disease prevention and healthy living. In the high school where I went there were 40 graduating, 25 of them girls. Of the 25, I was maybe the only one who did not have a parent in the United States, who did not receive remittances.

The high school was in Nombre de Jesús (*2.5 miles away*). I went to school there since 7th grade. In 7th grade here in Hacienda Vieja they were going to combine our class with the 6th grade, and we were going to have the same material as the year before, and I was not going to learn anything.

Now, I am active in the community. In Guarjila, I give a confir-mation class, I work with a group of special education children in a Rehabilitation Center, and I am very involved with a theater group there—the theater group goes out to all the remote communities.

Going to the university, at first I was going to study nursing, but I decided on social work—working with the people, not solving their problems but work with them on solving them, sharing, help-ing out as I can—I'm in love with social work.

My father had told us since childhood that he wanted a better future for us, but the reality of paying for school is difficult. My dad, he does work his piece of land, but we are supported by his job as a Health Promoter, and he is 57. He is scared that he is going to get replaced by a younger person. I have a brother in the United States, and I talked to him last week. He told me that he could not help me with costs of college as he now has a family of his own to support.

Update—January 2014: I live full-time in Guarjila now. I am a member of the ADESCO (*Community Development Association*). I continue working with the youth theater group and also as a volunteer for the local low-frequency radio station. I also was involved with a project that brought drinking water to a remote community, with support from an organization in Spain.

I am still studying social work at Andrés Bello University, and will graduate in a year and a half. Then? Well, if I don't find work, I will continue volunteering here in this community.

Pedro

I met Pedro in Alexandria, Virginia in March 2012, through an anthropologist who had taught English in Pedro's home town in El Salvador. Compact and forceful, he was glad to share his experiences of coming to and living in the United States.

I grew up in Guarjila, in the state of Chalatenango in the northwest part of the country (*about 30 miles from Hacienda Vieja, where I have conducted research*). Nine years ago, when I was 18, I left El Salvador, two months before getting my high school degree. You see, my father, he had left earlier to come to the United States, but at that time he was not supporting us, not sending remittances down. He had another family in America, and was supporting them. My mother has some health problems, and the medicines are expensive, and I am her only source of support.

I tried twice to come to the United States, and it took me 40 days to get here. The first time, it was in an 18-wheeler shipping cattle. There was no air in the truck, and the smell of manure was overpowering. If the police had not stopped the truck, all of us inside would have died. The police took us back to the border of Mexico and Guatemala. Now, I was with a *coyote* (smuggler), and we immediately started heading through Mexico again. This time, we hid in a refrigerated truck with fruit. It was cold, but we were fine, and made it through the border without any problems.

I made it here to Northern Virginia—lots of Salvadorans here. I worked in construction until the recession in 2008, and since then, in restaurants. I have never had trouble finding a job—I'm a good worker with great work habits. I am illegal, undocumented, and for now I use a "gray ID." It's someone else's Social Security card and number. He's not working now, and he gave me permission to use it.

My dad, he's a permanent resident here, and he is helping me to apply for a green card, to be a permanent resident. But I don't know how long that will take. Will I ever go back to El Salvador? Not to live. I look forward to the time when I can go back and visit, but this is my home now. There are so many opportunities here.

Update: Pedro's father was able to get Pedro legal status in the United States. A Facebook post showed Pedro visiting back in Chalatenango in early 2014.

Rebeca

I have known Rebeca since 2005 through her employment at the Universidad Panamericana. In many ways she epitomizes the friendly and hard-working personality of Salvadorans.

I grew up here in San Salvador, in the Monserrat neighborhood until I was seven. That was my world at that time—my friends, my first school. But what I did not know then is that my mom rented that house and she dreamed of owning a home. Through a foundation, she had the opportunity to build a house in a neighborhood outside of the city of San Martín, half an hour from San Salvador if you are driving. It was a mutual aid project, in that a foundation provided the lot and she would work on building the house on Sundays. When we moved, it was a completely new experience—semi-rural, it used to be a coffee plantation, a new school, away from my friends. When we got there there was not a community center or school or health clinic. The buses did not reach there yet, so you had to walk into San Martín to catch the bus. At that time I felt such frustration but I could not change anything.

Since that move, we have always lived there—me and my mother. My father would sometimes visit us but never has supported us. Until she recently retired, my mother worked all this time in a *maquila (a factory in which raw materials are imported without tariffs, then manufactured and exported; in El Salvador, these are almost entirely for textiles)*. She supported me and paid for my school expenses, which were not great at that time.

I went to a 3-year high school there, the San Martín INSAM with an accountancy emphasis. I learned a lot in that place—so much that I wanted to keep studying at a university to define myself as a person.

I wanted to go the National University and had applied there—but I did not have a job or a way to afford going to college. And here I need to give thanks to God for a friend who one day was listening on the radio and heard that the Panamerican University needed a person to work in their small bookstore—making photocopies, selling school supplies, etc. At that time I did not even have the money to pay bus fare to go to UPAN if I got an interview or to print off a resume. My friend paid for the bus fare and helped me with the resume and printed it.

When I got to the Panamerican University, I was interviewed by the Vice-Chancellor in charge of Administration and Finance. She was—and is—a very friendly person. It was my first job interview—I was 19 years old and had never worked before. She interviewed 12 people for this job, some with much experience. She must have seen something, for a few days later they called me and told me I had the job.

I worked in the bookstore six months and then they asked me to be a receptionist. I did that for a year, doing office tasks as well. When the assistant to the accountant left, and I had knowledge in that area from my high school studies, they offered me the position. I have had increasing responsibility in this area over the years, in charge of purchasing and monitoring cash flow.

I studied part-time during these years. At times, with new responsibilities, I would have to stop studying for half a year, but the administrators adjusted my schedule so that I could take classes. In June, 2013, at the age of 30, I graduated with a college degree in business. Shortly after that, I was promoted to the position of general manager in the area of Administration and Finance.

My mother and I still live in San Martín. That neighborhood has gotten dangerous. I don't walk around the neighborhood, even on a Sunday to go to a basketball court or soccer field. And walking, you don't say "hi" to anyone. You don't know if they are connected to a gang and want to know where you live. Also, there is another gang who would like to extend their territory to here, and the gang members here are suspicious if you want to talk to them. They think if you are friendly that you are an informer or spy, trying to get information to pass on to the other gang. A few months ago I called Pollo Campero (*a fast-food restaurant, like KFC*) in San Martín and asked to have food delivered. When I gave the person my address, he said that they do not deliver to that neighborhood.

I would like to move to another neighborhood, maybe back to the Monserrat neighborhood where we once lived, someplace safer and closer to work. It is an hour and a half commute by bus each way, and I don't usually leave work until 6:30, so I am always getting home in the dark. My mother does not want to move, to sell the house—because of the violence, we could not get what the house is worth if we sold it. I tell her that I don't mind paying for the rent if we could live somewhere else.

I also want to keep learning, get a degree in financial management, maybe a Master's degree in economics. I want to learn how to drive and I'd like to travel, to get to Europe, to see the Vatican. Perhaps one day I will have a family.

Toribio, José, and Antonio

Since I came to El Salvador in 2005 as a Fulbright Scholar, I have been coming to a small hotel on the Pacific Ocean for a day almost every time I come down. When you live in Wisconsin, as I do, you need to take advantage of any chance you get to go to an ocean. The hotel, Roca Sunzal (www.rocasunzal.com), is located 45 minutes from the capital, San Salvador, where I stay, and is on one of the best surfing beaches on the Pacific Ocean. I don't surf, but I go there because you are right on the ocean, the rooms and the swimming pools are clean, the beer is cold, and you meet interesting people from all over the world.

Showing up there a couple of times a year, I have gotten to know the waiters and bartenders, so I asked them before coming down in 2013 if I could interview them for this book. Their accounts are here, and Toribio's description of his family leads off the chapter "Families." They are interesting guys. Toribio is slim and lithe, and moves with grace and a dazzling smile. José has a perpetually serious expression, the kind of conscientious employee that every employer wants. Antonio is a big guy, an imposing figure behind the bar.

Toribio

When I was growing up, my family was poor. We moved around a lot the first eight years, and after my parents separated, we lived in a tiny little house that a relative provided. Then we moved here to El Tunco (*a beach community*) because there was more work.

I started to work when I was 10, maybe younger. I would gather firewood to sell and worked the crops. We would get out of school in November, and I would be involved in harvesting corn for at least two months.

About that time I started to surf. I began with a boogie board, and I learned on it how to stop on the waves. Then a friend and I bought an old board. We would leave it near the point (*the best surfing spot in the area*) at the entrance to a cave, so that no one would steal it—but it was so old that no one would steal it anyway. Then I started to teach my sister to surf, and the two of us bought a better board. My sister—she got good, and won second place in a competition. She married a surfer from the United States, and they live in San Francisco now.

I have competed in surfing competitions, but I have never had the time to really train. Now, I am too old to be really competitive, but if I had trained hard 5 years ago when I was 22 or 23, well who knows how far I could have gone—but one has to make money to live.

I started working here at Roca Sunzal in 2003 or 2004. At that time I took up with the woman I am now married to; our daughter is five and will be going to school soon.

Surfers come here from all over the world. Other than serve them meals, I surf with them and show them the best spots to surf. They give me shoes, pants, even once a surfboard. Other than black pants and shoes for work, I have not bought clothes for work in years.

I have thought about being a guide for surfers, but it is not stable. Some surfers—they come from all over the world, but they want to pay you little for showing them around. I do the surf guide as a side job; they give me time off here to do it.

The community I live in—you buy small lots, and then you build your house. My mother lives nearby—a group from another country built the house on the lot my sister bought for her.

I am finishing our house little by little. When we first moved in, we did not have a secure door. Now, there is still work to do on the windows, and we need a fan, but it is fine.

How safe is my community? Once I got a note asking for money. So I went to someone that I knew was in a gang, and told him that I knew that he was a person of influence. I told him that I worked hard, that my daughter was sick then—how could I pay? I did not hear anything more about this, and you know, it might have been a neighbor who drinks too much. I had given him a shirt once when he asked, but when he also asked for a shirt for a friend, I refused. Other than that, I have had no problems. But when someone calls the police—they arrive two or three hours later—they are scared of the gang.

You ask me why I stay here rather than leaving for the United States. I have no desire to leave. My mother is here. Here I can surf. This beach—it is more tranquil than in other places, and I have a good job. There, in the United States, it is cold.

José

I have been working here at Roca Sunzal for 7 years. Before that—I cleaned fish on the big dock in La Libertad when I was 12, and washed dishes in a restaurant before starting to work as a waiter while I was in high school. It was a necessity. My father, he drank a lot, and then left when I was young. Finishing high school, I worked at a couple of other clubs and hotels before coming to Roca Sunzal.

I like working here. The tips are split among the waiters, the cooks, and other staff. There is a 10% tip added to all restaurant bills in this country, but in many places, the wait staff does not see any of that money. Plus, here they always pay you on time.

My wife cooks here at Roca Sunzal, and we have two children. We bought a lot in a community near here, but it will take us one or two more years to build a house there.

When the second child was born, you see, I was studying English, but then there was not enough money to keep studying; I like studying (*there was a wistful tone to his voice*). I also help my mother, and she is getting old and has bad knees and does not work anymore. I help pay her rent and the cost of her medicine—the meds are $60 a month.

I have a brother in the U.S., in Houston. He's there without papers, and does not earn much. At times he'll send $20 or $30. I'll stay here. The only important thing is to be close to your family. If I was there, I would not know how my mother is doing, how the boys are.

Antonio

I worked at another restaurant for 5 years before coming here a year and a half ago because the money is better, there are more foreigners here. Between my salary and share of the tips added on to the restaurant and bar bills, that's about $300 a month. But I also get tips from the patrons at the bar. On a really good night, that can be $25.

Now, I am married and have been married for 6 years. My wife is a nurse at a clinic in San Salvador, and we have two children. We are buying a small house.

Where we live in La Libertad, it's not that bad. There are a few gang members in the community, and my cousin was killed last year. No one knows by whom he was killed or for what reason. The big concern is taking the bus from La Libertad to here—it's not that far, but buses are not safe.

I was abandoned at the age of 9 months by my parents, raised by my grandparents, with some contact with my father. But then my grandmother died when I was 9, and I got passed around from relative to relative. At 10, I started taking drugs, robbing to pay for the drugs. When I was 11, though, I got a job at a bakery, and worked there through high school. I stopped taking drugs, and now do not take any drugs, and I don't drink.

I took a course in how to be a waiter when I got out of high school, and I have been a waiter and bartender since then. Here on the coast, there are lots of restaurants, lots of jobs.

I'd like to go to the United States, but only to visit, and only if I could go there legally. I have uncles and cousins there, in Maryland and Los Angeles. None of them have the connections to get me papers if I wanted to live there.

Maria Rosa

Through my co-researcher Virginia Quintana, I got connected to Maria Rosa, a Salvadoran returning college student.

I was born in Soyapango, a suburb of San Salvador (*population 300,000*). We lived in several neighborhoods there, and I still live there; my husband and I with our two children live with my mother. I live in a small urban neighborhood with electricity and water/sewage services. There are about 100 families here, and we all know each other. There are four storefront shops, like mini-marts for those who do not go to the downtown market—15 minutes on foot—and one family that bakes dinner rolls that they sell. A lot of the families have cars. Two private schools are nearby, one Catholic and the Evangelical Christian school where our two sons study.

It used to be a quiet neighborhood where children went out to play and people were not afraid to walk around at night. But about six months ago (*this interview was conducted in January 2014*) young gang members starting marking the walls of houses and buildings with gang graffiti, and things have changed.

I graduated from a technical high school with an emphasis on business and computers. On graduation, our mother explained to my sister and me that she could not pay for our going to college. I was really sad—I was an excellent student and now instead of going to college I needed to find work. That was in 1999, and I found a job and started work. I had met the man that I would marry and we married in July 2002. I was already expecting, and with the birth of our first son, I dedicated myself to the role of wife and mother.

While I did that wholeheartedly I never gave up my dream of continuing my studies. In January 2011, when I visited the health clinic of the City of Soyapango, I saw that the Panamerican University was offering the BEPAZE program. To me this was a blessing because I was sure that God was giving me a new opportunity. I talked with someone in the city government and that is how I was able to start my dream of entering college that same month. College for me, studying law, is personal and professional improvement, and I believe that it will improve the quality of life for my family and provide opportunities for my children to have a better education.

It's tough now economically because my husband spends months at a time out of work. The cost of food, of everything, is constantly increasing, and while he is skilled in the installation of air conditioning and all HVAC work, that is not paid well here. That is why my husband has seen the need to travel to Panama to work there.

It is a huge sacrifice because there is not only the physical distance but also the emotional distance between us when he is in Panama, and alone parenting. I do not have paid employment, but with helping my children with their studies, what needs to be done around the house and my college classes—it's wearing. I am almost always alone, fighting to keep us going as a family, but this is the only way to have the money to do what is necessary for our two little ones. It's difficult to come out ahead with all the costs and, you know, one learns how make a budget so that we can get by on what my husband makes.

Alejandro

I interviewed Alejandro in 2005, when he was 17 years old. He is the cousin of Andrés, whose account of going to first grade at age 15 is in the "Education" chapter. A little shy, he only wanted to talk about his plans for the future.

To tell you the truth, I do not know what will happen in the future. My father is sick, and I am thinking of just studying for a technical degree and looking for a job. But my interests are in the sciences, in being a scientist. I could become a pharmaceutical chemist. I like this area very much, and that is a career that is available in El Salvador, but I really prefer research in technology and biology. In technology, the most up-to-date breakthroughs, and research on the latest advances in medicine. To be involved in looking for a cure for some disease like AIDS or cancer—I always want to find out about this.

(I asked what he does in his spare time). I think, kind of in the research method. I make some notes, about what comes to me. For instance, why some people have pimples on their face. I wonder if this happens for X reasons, if the reason is because the skin is too oily or there are bacteria. Well, I start writing some hypotheses and I write a lot about it in a small notebook.

(In 2012, I went to Ilobasco to interview Alejandro again, and asked him what he had been doing since graduating high school.) I got a technical degree at Andrés Bello University, in computers. It was working with computers and programming, and we learned to how to seek out more information when we needed it, to be seekers of information. I graduated in 2010, two years ago.

I have been looking for a job that is stable, one where I could develop my abilities, one where I would be doing something for society. I worked for a year in the ITCA *(Technical Institute of Central America, a for-profit institution).* So I was part-time, teaching classes in computers, but getting paid only for the hours that I taught. We were expected to recruit people to take classes—marketing, but we were not paid for this. We had to be there all week long, and did not even make the minimum wage.

So I left there in 2011, and it's been about a year since I had work. I am thinking about getting a certificate that you need to teach computers in the schools. Even though I have this technical degree, I would need this certificate—and that would take a year, and if I get this, and if there were jobs of this kind here, I would be able to get them.

I have an idea about the future, about a business in the Internet, like Facebook, but not as massive. If I could do that, I would have money to be able to help people here.

Although it is difficult here, I have no desire to leave El Salvador. How do you say it—I have roots here. A part of it is family. My mother is here—I live with her. My father, he is in the United States—Houston, I think. I have not talked with him in maybe 5 months.

Rooted—the other part is the church, is God. I know that I am meant to be of service that I can give to God. I am involved in a vocal group, and we are using it, we are hoping that this brings youth into the church. The idea—to show them that life is different with God in your life. A lot of youth, they are just not aware, wandering around, they could get killed. To show them that there are other ways to struggle, to strive to get ahead. In spite of the situation here, I will stay here.

You see, here with kids as young as 13, if they don't have direction from the church, or from a philosophy of life, they can become delinquent and hurt the community instead of being a part of the community. Without that guidance, that idea of another way to live, they will grow up robbing, and may die young.

The violence here, it has not affected me directly, but there is not a sense of tranquility. To go out at night—no, I don't do that. But I will stay here in El Salvador, in Ilobasco.

Blanca

In 2005, when I was in Ilobasco, a small city in the center of El Sal-vador, conducting interviews for my documentary Difficult Dreams, I interviewed one of the staff members at Mojé Casa Artesenal (or Casa Mojé), a non-profit that works on issues of youth and violence and which employs youth and ex-gang members in the production of high-quality handicrafts. It was suggested that I interview Blanca, a 24-year-old former gang member who worked there. As the following interview indicates, the non-profit was instrumental in her reshaping her life. I also found out later that struggles between the two gangs in Ilobasco had resulted in the leaders of both gangs being killed, and the lack of leadership made it much easier for gang members to leave at that point in time.

I am from Ilobasco, grew up here. For much of my life I have worked as a domestic servant, but for the last four years I have been at Casa Mojé.

When I was 15 years old, I joined a gang. Part of it was my family. I felt oppressed by them, felt discriminated against. They did not give me any opportunity to get out, to see places, to have friends. I felt, and you know, a lot of youth feel that way, to be in a poor family, to grow up that way, and your family does not support you. I believed that I needed more support from them, because at that age we need to have someone who is paying attention to us, someone who listens and talks to us.

I was 15 years old when I entered a gang. I do not know, but when someone who was born and grew up in a poor family, without any support, in the hard times that we face when we were young, the only way out seemed to be to enroll in a gang, and I did exactly that. I left my house and joined a gang.

Since the moment that I decided to leave my house, I slept in the street, in abandoned houses, nights and days that were wasted. I spent 6 months or so living that way.

Being in a gang—one does not know what will happen when one enters a gang. You are hungry, you get beaten by other gang members—and there is the way that other people treat you when they realize that you are a member of a gang.

It was difficult to leave the gang. By yourself, one cannot do it. When I had my first daughter, I tried to be less active in the gang. I wanted to do something else, and went to the market, but no one would give me work. There was discrimination, because they knew of my gang involvement. So I thought "If the society does not accept me, if I cannot find work, I will go back to the gang." With them, they supported me, and I felt safe, and with my companions.

I got married to another gang member and had another child. I left the children with my mother, and went back to the gang. Then individuals from Casa Mojé started hanging around with us. They considered us important, and they paid attention to us. In listening, I realized that there were doors that were open to us, that there could be an exit.

They offered workshops on how to develop ourselves, with movies and group discussions. They rented a house for us to meet and then provided lessons on how to do silk-screen printing. There also was a psychologist that we could meet with individually. Then one day they told me that I had been accepted into training to work on painting the handicrafts. You don't get paid when you are in training, but they gave me money for food. When there was an opening, I was employed to do the painting on the wooden handicrafts. And that is what I have been doing the last four years.

I really like painting! Also, depending on the sales, I can make $350-$400 a month, enough for me and my children. And not just the money. I have been taking courses on leadership, and I have taken a course on family violence—I have gotten involved in these things. And these have helped me to move forward. We want youth to know about their rights, and the right to speak out and make your own decisions.

My goal is to be a small business owner, to create a business for women, a place in which women could work.

Daniel

There are some neighborhoods in the big cities where people lock themselves in their houses when darkness arrives, and even in the day watchfulness to the point of hypervigilance is needed, where violence can affect actions that should be just part of being young, or being human. Danny Burridge, who lived and worked in La Chacra, a very low-income community in San Salvador (where I lived as a Peace Corps Volunteer decades earlier), writes movingly about one young man who he knew there.

I hesitated in writing this. It feels like I don't have the right to it. It is too fresh, it is an open gaping wound with only the first *curacion* applied. But I think it's important to name Daniel Castillo, to not give him a pseudonym. I mean, nothing can happen to him at this point.

I spent at least an hour yesterday talking to Luis, Daniel's best friend. Both of us straddled the little drainage ditch on the side of the *linea* while people noticed us talking about something important, and I tried to figure out what I could say about Daniel. Luis told me the story of how it all went down, how he just felt something was going to happen to Daniel. He pointed out the wall and the door that Daniel had possessively insisted on painting to make a few extra dollars. And finally, Luis told me to concentrate on the good stuff, although no one is all virtue, obviously. We all got complexities, defects, and Daniel had an awful lot. He was the one who forged his own destiny. And yet, somehow people loved him, Daniel let himself be loved. That was his gift.

I think it was when he got out of prison that we first started chilling and became friends. And I only say that after reflecting for a number of days. Amigo isn't a word lightly thrown around in El Salvador. I remember so clearly a day in November '09 getting off the bus at the *Castilleja* and turning down the *linea* towards the parish. I could see a familiar figure down the line in the near distance, with his shirt off scratching madly at his sides. I got closer and saw that it was Daniel, *el chicharrita*, the Little Cicada. Daniel's older brother was the *mero Chicharra*, very well known in the area. He got the name because when he was younger he would take a whiz absolutely wherever he felt like it, apparently just like a cicada. And so Daniel was the little brother, the little cicada. I got closer and saw that he had a horrible red rash all over his body that was pussing at various spots.

"Hey what's up Daniel!?"

"*Que ondas* Daniel?"

"You finally got out man! It's great to see you. How you doing?"

"*Puya* glad to be out, reformed man, you understand? But I got this itch inside too."

As he told me a little more about having been *preso*, I could tell he was reformed. When young kids go to jail in El Salvador, the vast majority come out worse, with new contacts, new ideas, a masters degree in crime as they say. But Daniel looked genuinely scared, desperate, and not just for the rash, but that he had lived things that he never wanted to repeat. And this from a kid who was always hard, who made an effort to keep you from wanting to mess with him.

"Damn man, I had thought you moved out of here or something, but then they told me that they took you. It's great that you're back. Don't scratch that thing man, you'll just spread it."

"Naw don't worry, the Niña Concha is going to give me a spice bath, I'll be fine. Hey, I need a job though, dog—we should see if you can give me a chance there at the Open School with the kids teaching drawing."

"Alright yeah, we'll see," I told him.

We exchanged some more words and I sighed to myself as I walked away, doubting that we could put an ex-convict in the mix to teach art to kids in a violence prevention project that was just finally getting off the ground.

I would see Daniel just about every day. His house was right along my route going into the parish. We'd greet, chat, chill a little bit, maybe buy some fruit from Hilda who had her little stand right where the passageway led down to the parish. And sometimes he would show up in the afternoon to the parish soccer court while the

Open School kids had their recreation. Every now and again, I tried to ask him why he had got sent to jail. He finally told me that he had taken the fall for a girl he liked who just happened to be carrying extortion money. Other people said it was for robbery, but Daniel assured me he had kicked that bad habit. And he would ask me about the States, and about the sports we play (he was one of the few basketball fans in La Chacra), about the girls there, about the buildings, the people who are artists for a living. He was curious, smart, raw, one of the youth that I most talked with. He would tell me all sorts of stories with so much trust, but I didn't always trust it all.

But one thing that was not debatable was his talent. He was an amazing artist. I first met him when I was still new in El Salvador, running delegations with SHARE. We would take the tour around the parish and often times he would be in the *Centro de Dia*, with the old folks and the *Maestra Milagro*, using the sewing machine, or helping to draw and paint the sheets that were used for the backdrop during masses. He would make tie-dyed shirts and sell them to the delegations that showed up, always with a smile and a joke. He was a charmer, happy to be alive, someone who gravitated towards you and you towards him.

One day as I was walking down the *linea* towards him he darted into his house and came out with something in his hand. As soon as I was in arm's reach he plopped a super-stylish gray mesh-back Texaco baseball cap onto my head. "Hey, I'm sick of you showing up with that shaggy hair all wind-blown all over the place. Looks like you haven't showered in days." The ladies who were gathered around the fruit stand giggled and politely said I looked good in it.

"Hey thanks man, I'll give it back when I head out today."

"*N'ombre*, it's yours…if you're going to actually wear it that is. If you really don't want it, you give it back, cause I'll rock it."

"Alright," I said. "I'll take it then, and I'll get you a hat to replace this one, from Cincinnati, we got some good ones."

"Sounds good," he responded.

Around mid-June of this year, Xiomara finally convinced me to let Daniel come give the drawing and painting workshops in the Open School. Aside from sometimes showing up late, or not at all, he did an excellent job. He taught the kids how to do landscapes with different layers of distance, how to shade using colored pencils, how to use pastels to make fruit, flowers and clowns just like Sister Patty had taught him. One day when he was trying to think of what to teach them, he suddenly said "ah I got it," and went running out of the Open School. Xiomara and I passed about 10 exasperated minutes trying to entertain the kids and inwardly complaining about Daniel's unreliability. But then he showed up panting, with an arm full of flat dirty rocks that he had gotten from the banks of the river. "Alright kids, grab a rock and wash it off in the *pila*." Within the hour the kids all had beautiful mountainous landscapes painted onto their personalized rocks which would have wet the mouth of any *artesania* fan.

But after a few months, some folks around the parish started murmuring about how Daniel wasn't the one who should be helping out in the Open School, setting the example for our young impressionable kids. He was too loose with his words, with his behavior in the community, he was just trying to take advantage of the parish and he had already been given so many chances. As much as I tried sticking up for him, saying that no one could give better art classes, I couldn't refute the behavior argument. So when we started up the Open School again this November, it fell to me to let him know we wouldn't need his services anymore. As soon as I started a pretty classic Salvadoran beat-around-the-bush and let-him-down-easy talk, he said "ah, I already get it. And who was it?"

"Who was what?" I asked.

"Who is it that doesn't want me around?" he said with only a mildly threatening tone.

"Well, it was lots of people. They say you don't set a good example."

"And how am I supposed to set a good example if I can't be around?"

Very clever, but somehow not convincing enough. He didn't wait for an answer though, and split.

Despite our decision, during the past month or so he would randomly show up to the Open School space for the recreation hour, when I am normally up with kids at the soccer court. And he would listen to music with kids, teach them some modern dance moves. When I would come in and see him there, I wouldn't talk to him. He probably thought he was going about setting a good example, but showing up when we had told him not to wasn't a good start. I could feel him wanting to talk sometimes, but didn't he realize I would have to say to him: "damn man, what are you doing here?" So I delayed the conversation, I looked the other way. I remember the now-wretched feeling of the last day I saw him, walking out of the door of the Open School as I turned away from him to pick up a candy wrapper off the floor.

I never really wore the Texaco hat much. I didn't like repping a big destructive gas company no matter how stylish and comfy the hat was. Just the other week, I finally decided to give it back to Daniel, so he could switch up with his black Reds hat and sleek gelled Mohawk. I thought it might even be a good way for me to bridge the silent treatment gap that I had created between us. So I brought it to the Open School and put it on top of the cabinet where we store all of our materials to wait for him to show up. But he didn't show up. I should've known that you don't give back gifts.

On the morning of Thursday, December 9th, I found myself in the *cocina* with Niña Estela there within the parish. She said she would tell me some gossip, that Daniel had gone missing, since Monday, and that some people were saying that he was dead. His family had put in the *denuncia* the previous day. I was shook up, but blew it off. "Yeah he's like that, he just goes off on his own sometimes, he'll turn up...but I hope he's alright."

Just a couple hours later, the information was suddenly flying around the parish. It was true. *Medicina Legal* had called the family to let them know that it was indeed Daniel who had been found near the *Cornucopia in el Centro,* with cuts on his face and numerous bullet wounds in his chest.

Apparently it had been for the same girl that he had gone to jail for. Maybe he really loved her. He had gone to her house to take her out on the town with the money from painting Luis's wall. The problem is that Daniel lives in La Chacra, one of the most notorious 18 territories in all of San Salvador, and she lives in La 22 de Abril, a couple neighborhoods over, one of the most notorious MS-13 territories in all of San Salvador. Word is she might have been a *marero's* girlfriend too. So he shouldn't have gone, he broke the rules. He knew he was risking his life, especially given who his brother is, but it's not like that justifies it.

I'm currently listening to Reggaeton and thinking of how much Daniel loved to dance and thinking he would probably be wanting us to dance and party in his honor. So I try not to be sad, but it still doesn't seem real. It's more like maybe he just disappeared for a while again, or maybe he got sent to jail again. I mean I need to reconcile with him still, tell him I'm sorry for not talking to him, tell him how much I appreciate him, tell him I can't wait until he's a famous Salvadoran painter. And now I can't, and I'm torn up.

But my regret and sadness is nothing compared to the pain of his family and those who loved him. They cry and mourn, and invite their distant relatives in to town to cry with them, and they walk up and down the *linea* asking for a few cents from the inhabitants of each shack to help pay for the wake. Luis talks about him like he's still just right there down the *linea* and will probably show up any minute to look for something to paint. He even looks in the direction of Daniel's house with his eyes extra squinted against the sun and the memories. But he laughs at how many *dolares* Daniel hoodwinked him out of over the years, and smiles at how there haven't been that many people at someone's wake in a long time.

Everyone is pulling out our mechanisms to deal with never again seeing someone who you used to see every day. Everyone says it's a shame, it's so sad, he was so young, 23, just a kid. And some people go on saying he was a bad piece, he was involved in shady things, no one is exempt from anything in this country. He went into the 22 de Abril for God's sake. And people cope, because they have no other choice. The pain that they carry in their heart is often times not visible, but we all share it, we all know it's there.

This past week in the Open School, our last week of the year, we were working on the topic of hope with the kids. One day they had to express personal answers to a number of questions in front of the whole group. One of the questions was what do you hope for in your life. I was stunned at how many of the kids expressed that they hoped that they and their families would stay alive, that they would continue living. Some laughed as they said it, some were stone grim, but I knew it because of Daniel. Violence and death are always on the tip of everyone's tongue, shivering down everyone's spine, constant variables. But I knew this was probably the first time for a lot of kids that someone they had known closely, someone they had danced with, learned how to paint with, maybe learned a dirty joke with, had been killed. And they just didn't want it to happen to them. It's the bare bones of hope. Your deepest, most profound, most heartfelt hope is just to keep living, and sometimes it's hard to grasp that type of hope, let alone get happy about it. But it makes life more beautiful, it makes you appreciate life more, and especially appreciate those who will only live on in our hearts.

Que descanses en paz Chicharrita…(Rest in peace, Little Cicada). It shouldn't be this way.

Luís

I met Luis Figueroa a few years ago through a mutual friend who also works in the area of conflict resolution.

I am 31 years old, a lawyer, and work for the justice system, in the area of alternative conflict resolution. I have been working in this area for 8 years—it was a part of my studies in my undergraduate years. (*Note: In El Salvador, as in much of Latin America, a law degree is an undergraduate, not a graduate degree.*) I had done my thesis on conflict resolution, and a few months after graduating, I got the job.

My mother lives in California. She has been there since 1994. I stayed here, taking care of my grandmother. Most of my family lives in California—in Los Angeles and San Francisco. I was 14 or 15 when my mother left because we needed the income. Since moving to California, she has remarried. When she got there, she began the process of legalization, and now she is a citizen. When she got permanent resident status, she asked me if I would like to come to the United States through the policy of family reunification, and I said "no." I have been to San Francisco where she lives, as a tourist, and she has asked me other times if I want to come to the United States, and my response has always been "no."

I knew that there were other things that I needed to do here as well as take care of my grandmother. When I decided on my career, it was with the idea of staying here, never of leaving. There is the potential of helping other people to improve access to the judicial system here. The ideal of justice in this country always has been somewhat removed from the actual situation. This I saw as a challenge when I started studying. I first thought about being a doctor—I think because of the idea of helping people. When I realized that I couldn't stand the sight of blood, I decided to change to be a lawyer, to help others without dealing with blood.

So what I tell friends, "If you want to help, to be of service, this is one of the best places in the world to do so. Around the corner, there are problems to be solved, issues to be overcome." This is marvelous in that it is a chance to serve and to develop myself. This is my country. Others have had to leave—for the war, for economic reasons—my family members had to leave, but they left a part of their heart here. Therefore, I wanted to aid this country where my family has its roots. I aim to do what I can so that others do not have to leave the country.

I live in San Marcos (*an urban community 20 miles from San Salvador*). The impression is that San Marcos is a very dangerous area. I guess that this comes from police statistics, and yes, there are a lot of youth who have come into conflict with the police. My experience, and I have lived 16 or 17 years in San Marcos, is that in my neighborhood there are gang members. I talk with them and I know them. They tell me, "You know, we are from the MS-18. But don't worry—in this neighborhood nothing happens." In our neighborhood, there is not one sign of graffiti, not on any wall. There is an agreement between the gang and the *directive (elected community group)* that the community will be peaceful. I have forgotten to lock my door at times, and nothing has ever happened. I left the window down in my car one night, and a gang member knocked on my door to tell me this. It's like, these youth have entered into the gang but they continue to be neighbors.

Through social media, through the Internet, more than a year ago, I met other youth with similar thoughts, who share the hope to live in a country better than it is now. It is a movement of youth who want to express yourself, not just to voice your opinion, but to participate in change. There is a craving to put into practice what we learned in college—and to demand changes that are congruent with our ideals.

There was an event, when the legislature was going to intervene in the composition of the Supreme Court. Especially, through Twitter and Facebook, people were speaking out against this. Many of us knew that this was against our ideals and against the Constitution. Someone would post an idea, and another would add onto it and share it. This went on building, with many youth participating and finally, someone said: "Let's take to the streets." This was not something that most of us had done before—I had never done this before. We marched in front of the President's House to express our opinion about this, and this was followed by other outpourings. (*Note: according to news accounts and persons familiar with the situation, the outpouring of youth was a prime reason why the legislature reversed its actions on the Supreme Court.*)

This was the beginning of a new platform for activism for youth. It was not just the networks of social media but a way to translate that into physically connecting us one with another, to find out what each was doing for the country, all with one common theme of trying to do what was just, what was right for the country.

Since then, we continue in contact, we get together from time to time, and there are plans for the future. One idea is to form a group to come up with alternative plans—neither from the right or the left. We consider ourselves political, but not political in terms of the political parties, ARENA or the FMLN. This initiative aims to come up with alternative plans, to come up with new ideas, to claim a space for these ideas, for no one will give this to us if we do not demand it ourselves.

These new methods of communication offer us connectedness. There are many young Salvadorans who do not live in El Salvador but who are concerned about the country and offer support to those who live here. Youth wherever we live have the ability to work the technology, to find out information, to disseminate it. This is a new role for youth, the diffusion of ideas.

We are connected with people all over the world, Salvadorans who do not live here but who are concerned about the country. This connectedness and the online communities that we had formed served the country well with the latest natural disaster, Tropical Depression 12-E in September 2011, and we set about trying to respond to this new disaster. We called out to people in other countries to ask for money for supplies to take out to the communities. From as far away as Salvadorans living in Japan came money which we used to buy food, which we transported and distributed in three communities affected by the flooding.

Many of us have this desire to pay back to the country. A lot of us have been able to finance our education through money sent back from relatives in the United States. The challenge for us, for the country, is how to improve the educational system and how to engage those of us who are educated, and use the support that comes from the United States to open up spaces where young people can be successful. To find spaces, to be a link for others is the challenge. When we know ourselves, when we are connected—this is a powerful potential tool for benefitting the country.

Elisa

Through meeting with non-profit organizations who work with youth, I encountered Elisa. I've included her story as she represents the "reverse diaspora," the small number of young Salvadorans who, after living legally in the United States, have decided to return to El Salvador.

My mother migrated to the United States in 1984, when I was 7 months old. I was raised by my maternal grandmother. We lived in Mejicanos (*an urban area close to San Salvador*) until I was about 7 years old. By then, my mother had saved some money and bought a small house in in San Salvador. The house was in an urban area for low- to middle-income families. Houses were small, in rows (*alleys*) of about 16 houses facing each other, so everyone knew everything about each other. In a way it was nice because it felt like we were all looking out for each other. At least in my *pasaje* (*alley*), when my grandmother had to leave my cousins and me alone for a few days, our neighbors would keep a watch on us and report to her on all of our movements, which was sometimes a little bothersome. My favorite area in that *colonia* (*neighborhood*) was the basketball court where I spent a lot of time with my friends. The neighborhood was safe; people knew each other and their families. I lived there until I was 17 years old, and it was really hard for me when I had to leave.

It is very different than where I live now, a nearby apartment complex but everyone kind of does their own thing. One of my aunts still lives in that community and I love it when I go visit them and see all my neighbors, and my friends' kids, etc.

Growing up, I did all my schooling at a private Christian school. Private education in El Salvador does not necessarily mean good or high quality. This particular school, of which there are between 30–40 sites across the country, provides an alternative to public schools for "worried Christians," like my grandma, who want to ensure a Christian upbringing for their kids, and it is reasonably affordable.

Upon graduating from high school in 2001, I moved to the U.S. My mother, who had migrated illegally there in 1984, had become a U.S. citizen and done the paperwork to petition me. Even though

I was excited to see my mother, I hesitated to move because I did not want to leave my friends and grandma. Nonetheless, I thought it would be a good opportunity that would help me in the future, so I left, knowing that I would eventually return to El Salvador.

In the United States, my mother enrolled me at an ESL program in a local high school. After a year of studying ESL, I enrolled in my first college classes at Cerritos Community College, a 2-year institution. From there I was able to transfer to the University of California-Berkeley. That transition, from Cerritos College to UC-Berkeley was difficult—this was the first time I was completely out "on my own" and also, Cerritos College had a large Latino population, which was not the case for UC-Berkeley. I was blessed that although small, the Latino community was organized and there were several opportunities to be together and support each other. I graduated in 2006 with an undergraduate degree in Political Science. I do not have any pictures of my graduation because I did not attend the Commencement ceremony. I was thrilled to have reached such an accomplishment, but I was also sad I could not share with my family that moment since they couldn't possibly be there. I guess I've left out a very important, however tragic, event that took place which changed my life on so many levels. In July of 2002, almost two years after I moved to the U.S., my mother and sister were murdered at our home in Los Angeles. I thought about returning to El Salvador as soon as possible, but the thought of my mother sacrificing all this time for me so that I could have a better future, influenced me to stay and study hard.

The whole time in school I was also a volunteer. I volunteered for the YWCA, with youth at risk, mentoring, because I was always drawn to working with children and youth. After I graduated I moved to Brooklyn, New York, and worked there as a career counselor and social worker for three and a half years and then decided it was time to come back.

I had always planned on coming back to El Salvador. When I wrote my essay for admissions to UC-Berkeley, I stated that I wanted to pursue higher education to gain the knowledge, skills, and connections that would eventually enable me to come back to my country and contribute positively to its development.

In 2011 I returned. I came back with the idea of only staying for a year, while I figured out what the next steps would be. I wanted to go back to school for my Masters, but also wanted to see what was going on in the country, if I was going to be able to live here again, etc. You see, I lived in the States for ten years. It took a little bit of time to adjust back.

There were adjustments. In the U.S., I was on my own for the most part, and here, with family, when you are with them, they always ask a lot of questions. Where are you going? Who are you going with? When are you coming back? Etc. Questions I was not used to answering to anyone in the U.S. My grandma was now living in the countryside, in Morazán, so I lived with my aunt and her kids for a little over a year until I was able to get a job and rent my own apartment.

One of the adjustments has to do with the sense of insecurity here. Shortly after I came back, I was out with a friend one night, only until about 11:00 p.m., and we left our phones in his car. When we got back to the car, there were 15 missed calls on my phone from my aunt, the one I was living with, who was worried and wondering where I was and what had happened to me. She even went out to Santa Tecla (*a nearby city*) looking for me. My friend, who is an American, had almost the same number of missed calls on his phone from his friends who were also worried about him. We were fine, nothing had happened to us. When I got home everyone was mad at me for being insensitive to the security situation of the country. This was one of the main reasons I moved out on my own as soon as possible. My grandmother still calls me at random times, sometimes when I'm asleep, just wanting to make sure that I am okay.

Soon I started looking for opportunities to volunteer and an uncle, who is a teacher at a public school, told me about an organization called Glasswing International. I signed up to volunteer as a basketball coach for their after-school programs in schools. It was the first time I was volunteering in my own country, with girls that reminded me a lot of me when I was their age. Soon there was an opportunity to work at Glasswing and I stayed. It's a perfect job. The programs and clubs—there are chess clubs, and science, and English, and sports—all these enrichment opportunities that, without Glasswing and all the volunteers who become positive role models, students from public schools would not have access to.

The program helps the students—in some cases makes them excited about school—and it also helps the volunteers. We are getting volunteers from universities, from professionals, as well as corporate volunteers. For many of the volunteers, who come from families with money, this is the first chance they have had to interact with those from poor communities, and we are changing minds. It's a big commitment, twice a week for six months to a year, and we are finding that there are a lot of Salvadorans who want to be involved in helping their country.

I never want to live anywhere else. Perhaps I will go back to the U.S. to continue my education. In the meantime, I intend to stay here and hopefully inspire other kids to continue studying and instill in them a little bit of hope. This country is worth it—so many opportunities to do things here and have real impact. We can't afford to let our young bright and strong youth leave the country. We need them here.

FORCES

5

Family

When I arrive at the small beachfront hotel and restaurant Roca Sunzal, one of the waiters, Toribio, always greets me with a smile: "Santa Claus!" I don't think I look much like Santa, but I am older with white hair, and anyway, it is always good to see Toribio. He is an athletic-looking 28-year-old, a surfer who has been a contender in surfing competitions. Before my 2013 trip, I had been in touch with him to ask if he would take some time to talk with me about his life and his family. As I listened to him describe his family situation, the complexities and transnational aspect of families in El Salvador became very apparent.

He started by talking about his mother, in her 50s, who now is not working; she takes care of the three teenaged children of Toribio's sister, who now lives in San Francisco. The sister, who has legal immigration status in the United States, sends money for her mother and the three children, and bought a small lot (for a house) for them; an international non-profit organization built a house for them a few years ago on that lot. She is the oldest of three sisters that Toribio has in the United States. The middle sister is undocumented, with a 2nd-grade education, and struggles to get by. The youngest sister, younger than Toribio by a couple of years, started surfing at the same time that he did. She excelled at surfing as she did at school, graduating first in her high school class. Like Toribio, she competed in surfing competitions in El Salvador. There she met a surfer from San Francisco, and they ended up marrying and moving to San Francisco, where they have two children.

Toribio lives with his wife and their 6-year-old daughter in a lower-middle-class community in a house that he built, a few houses away from his mother.

His situation illustrates "family life" in El Salvador. You can observe what we typically think of as a family—Toribio, his wife, and daughter. Also somewhat typical is the importance of proximity to family—children living close to their parents when they can. In this situation, you also see an example of transnational families—a family whose members live in more than one country. Like most Salvadoran transnational families, members who are living abroad send money when they can (the middle sister is not able to) and grandparents and other relatives often take care of youth.

In the four chapters that comprise this section on forces affecting youth, the last part of each chapter focuses on how its topic both supports and limits youth. In this chapter, I will start by discussing transnational families, which is by far the largest change in Salvadoran family structure over the past 40 years, and a family form not familiar to many American readers. I will also explore the difficulties in parenting in an atmosphere of violence.

Transnational families are prevalent in El Salvador, Mexico, and many other developing countries because all nations are now living in a world made smaller by globalization. In this first part of the 21st century, capital, goods, people, electronic communication, and media travel across national borders much faster than before. In this process, the nature of migration itself has changed. While the next chapter examines the overall changes brought about through migration in El Salvador and how this affects youth, the impact on families in particular is discussed here.

Citing political economist Saskia Sassen, Rhacel Salazar Parreñas writes that "nation-states maximize production in the global economy by lifting borders and welcoming the flow of capital, information, and labor but simultaneously closing these borders when it comes to the permanent integration of immigrants and refugees." As one speaker at a conference on immigration I attended said, "We wanted workers and we got people." People have families, and when there is considerable distance between parents and children, transnational families are created. Manuel Orozco defines transnational families as:

> *People who send and receive money create families that are separated by distance and reunited by love and the material circumstances that keep them in touch. They become transnational families by virtue of such separation and commitment, and represent different backgrounds. In this sense, a transnational family is a unit with household members across borders that stay in regular contact to maintain their bonds and responsibilities.*

By definition, a transnational family does not have to be one where family members cannot see one another from time to time. If your family is in Milan, Italy, and you are working in Geneva, Switzerland, you are only 200 miles apart, less than 4 hours by train. Traveling across borders in the European Union is not a problem as long as you have a passport from a European Union country. However, approximately half of the Salvadorans in the United States are undocumented, and getting across borders to visit their families is essentially impossible. They would have to make the more than 2000-mile trip to El Salvador twice, with not only the dangers of the trip but also the uncertainty of being able to get back across the border again safely.

A prime reason for Salvadorans to migrate is to support their families. According to the 2007 census, 21% of the households in the country receive remittances from a family member working abroad. In a 2009 survey, 28% of the youth stated that they received remittances. (As the impact of remittances cuts across so many facets of the life of youth, material on remittances is included in Appendix A).

Leisy Abrego, a Salvadoran-born professor at UCLA, makes the case that youth whose mothers have emigrated fare better than those whose fathers had emigrated. The lens of gender helps explains this. While women immigrants generally are in less well-paid positions than their male counterparts, Salvadoran mothers are more likely than the male parents to send large proportions of their often-meager earnings back to their children. As Abrego writes:

> To do this, they make extreme sacrifices, eating very little or sleeping on the floor in a small rented space. Griselda, a transnational mother, recalled the hardships she underwent when she first got a job in the United States.
>
> "I've always sent $300 [each month] to my [daughter], and I would get paid $100 weekly [working as a live-in nanny]. I would end up with $90 because I also had to pay the fee to wire the money. ... It was horrible. ... Each week I would buy a dozen ramen noodle soups, which I don't even want to see anymore, really. ... But I was the happiest woman in the world because my daughter had something to eat."

While women approach parenting as a strong commitment and—as seen in the quote above—put their child's or children's well being above their own, fathers often equate parenting responsibilities with marital relationships. When the marriage or partnership ends, often with the start of a new relationship, the sense of responsibility toward their child or children can also cease.

When I came to El Salvador in 2005, I heard transnational families referred to as "disintegrated families." These families were blamed for the delinquency of youth and their joining gangs and also, because of the presence of remittances, of being lazy and unwilling to work. As there was little research on the impact of parents living abroad on the youth left in El Salvador, I wanted to get a better understanding of this.

At the Universidad Panamericana de El Salvador, I taught a class in which the focus was a qualitative research project on perceptions of youth who had at least one parent working in the United States. The students in the class were trained in interviewing and then conducted interviews with youth they knew who had at least one parent living abroad. In order to interview as representative a group as possible, the students attempted to interview all the youth they knew who were in this situation. One of the advantages of the interviewers only interviewing persons known to them was that they were able to talk about sensitive issues, such as the emotional reactions of the youth when the parents left.

The Universidad Panamericana appeals to working adults, mostly from low-income and working-class neighborhoods or communities. Their classes are held on nights and weekends, and students often travel a long distance to get to them. Consequently, when I asked students to interview teens they knew in their own area, there was a geographical dispersion—4 of the 14 departments (states) and 11 municipalities were represented in the 33 youth interviewed. This research led to my development, with Virginia Quintana, of the monograph *Una Familia, Dos Paises (One Family, Two Countries: Understanding the Impact on Youth When Their Parent(s) Emigrate to the United States)*.

Working with the students in the class to analyze the qualitative data after the interviews were complete, I became aware of the strengths in many of these transnational families, and how many of the opportunities that the youth had were connected to the parent or parents working outside the country. I realized that it made more sense to think of the functions that any kind of family structure can provide than to only focus on the failings of transnational families, where the parents are not physically present for their children.

Although family structures vary, according to family scholar Nijole Benokraitis, most families fulfill five important functions: they legitimize sexual activity, they bear and raise children, they offer emotional support, they provide economic security, and they establish family members' places in society. I want to demonstrate how transnational families carry out the last four of these family functions.

In the area of bearing and raising children, one important aspect is setting and enforcing standards of behavior. This is an area in which transnational families may be somewhat deficient. Slightly more than half (53.1%) of the youth in the *One Family, Two Countries* study have lived without at least one parent for more than 9 years, and without the rules that those parents might have imposed. A number of these reported that if their parents returned, they would not have the freedom that they now enjoy. One 18-year-old female explained "If she were to come back, I could not go out the way I do now. I have a lot of liberty, and I don't want to lose this," and one 14-year-old male said "If my mother were to come back, she would restrict the freedom I have now, and it would not be the way it is now." This may indicate that the grandparents, aunts and uncles, and older siblings with whom the youth live are not as strict as the parents would be.

While some youth relish the lack of parental control, others may not have the structure and support that they wish for. This quote from Parreñas, on a study done of transnational families in the Philippines, seems applicable to El Salvador: "In addition to poor guardianship, children in two-parent-abroad transnational families also find themselves with the greater responsibility of having to manage the distribution of the emotional labor of their guardians. They fear overburdening kin with the responsibility of securing their emotional well-being." Parreñas adds, "children do not always feel that extended kin can be expected to provide as much care as would a parent."

However, in many families in El Salvador, with the parent or parents working long hours or two jobs to make ends meet, there is not much supervision of the youth. It also seems to me that some of the criticism of transnational families is based on comparison between the ideal family in El Salvador and the current transnational families. The ideal family does not always exist. I often hear Salvadoran men referred to as *pica flor,* as they stay with a woman and their children for a few years and then, like a bird that goes from flower to flower, they "fly away" and form another family. While it is not a representative sample, if you look at the family of origin of the eleven young adults in the "Stories" chapter for whom there is information, four of them came from two-parent families in El Salvador, four from single-parent families in which the absent father was living in El Salvador, and three from transnational single-parent families. Two of these youth lived with grandparents while growing up, while the mother worked and sent home money to them; the third emigrated to the United States to send money home to his mother.

Connected both to setting and enforcing behavior and offering emotional support is the contact that a child has with the parent or parents. Among the youth in transnational families interviewed for *One Family, Two Countries,* I was surprised by the amount of communication between the adolescents in El Salvador and their parents in the United States. Fully 71.0% of the youth reported contact with their parent or parents at least every 6–8 days. Four of the youth also reported communicating with their parent(s) by email. An example of frequent communication is the following: "We talk and write emails—we do that a lot. I feel that the communication with them (*the parents*) is good and I talk about all my issues and even joke. I talk about my studies, what I'm doing, if I need anything. They also give me much advice—that I behave myself, take care of myself, not go out at night alone."

In all of the cases reported, the parents were asking about the health/well-being of the students and family members. An example of this is: "She talks with me on the phone every eight days, tells me to behave myself, take care of my little sister, haul water, take care of her mother, and do well in school."

In a more recent study on transnational communication, Benitez confirmed the extent of communication and provided information on the substance of the communication between transnational family members. In-depth interviews with those aged 15–25 with family members living abroad documented that the conversations centered around their studies or their work (depending on whether or not they were in school), their behavior and activities, and also inquiries about family and community life—about how relatives were doing, about new babies, about festive days. The problems with personal safety were also a topic of conversation. In this study, some had said that the trust that they had with their parents had diminished while others said that it was the same. Several said that they sensed a need on the part of the family members living abroad to be of emotional support, to be a part of the family.

The same study also shows the rapid evolution of technology and its impact on family communication. Skype was being used regularly, and one youth said that when he does not have time to talk, he messages on Facebook to let them know that he is okay.

In communication between parents in the United States and children (and their caretakers) in El Salvador, the financial support through remittances is often central ("There will be a deposit on Friday,"). There is power that the parents have in providing the economic support. A parent can say, "I will only send you money if you stay in school," or, "If your grandmother tells me that you are not obeying the rules that we set for you, I will not send money directly for you."

However, the young person back in El Salvador also has power. Bri Erger, a Peace Corps Volunteer living in a remote village, told me of an exchange she had with two teen girls there. Peace Corps Volunteers are provided enough money to live on the same level as the residents in the area in which they were living, and these girls were wondering why this *gringa* did not have more money to go into the city and buy things. One asked, "You talk to your parents, don't you?" The Peace Corps Volunteer realized that behind the question was the assumption that if you talk (or agree to talk) with your parents, they will send you money.

Another function of families, according to Benokraitis, is to provide emotional support. In the *One Family, Two Countries* study, more than 70% of the youth interviewed mentioned more than one source of emotional support. The support came from the parent(s) in the U.S., from mothers when the father was working abroad, and from grandparents, uncles and aunts, and siblings. In only one case were friends mentioned as a major source of support. This comment illustrates the breadth of support that many youth have: (*the support comes*) "from my mother living in the U.S., from my brothers and sisters, from my aunt and grandmother."

In only 4 of the 30 cases did the youth not express feeling sadness when the parent(s) left. In three of these situations, the youth stated that they were too young to understand what had happened. The fourth was a situation in which the father who left had not spent much time with the youth before leaving. The following responses of the youth are representative of the way they felt on the parent leaving:

- *"I felt bad not being able to count on help from my own mother. I spent a lot of time in which nothing could cheer me up. There was something deep down that would not let me be calm."*

- *"We felt bad and I remember that when we were little I cried a lot. I was so attached to my father and I missed him so much. He would play with me, letting me ride on this back, and I enjoyed that so much! Even though I was little, I felt really sad."*

- *"I missed her. I thought that I would never see her again."*

In the great majority of the situations, the youth indicated that after the initial separation they have felt much better. The first youth quoted above answered the question "How do you feel now?" with: "Now, things seem very different to me because what I felt before I don't feel now because I have been able to overcome the emptiness that at first I was feeling."

A third function of families, says Benokraitis, is economic security, and it is clear that the remittances from abroad, which all the youth in this study received, provided this tangible support and security. An emotional impact, measured in feelings of security and reduced worry due to the money from the remittances, was mentioned by 57% of the respondents. In many of the cases, this was contrasted with how they felt when the parent(s) first left:

- (When he left): *"very bad—I cried every night";* (now): *"I feel good because we talk a lot (by phone) and he tells me that things are going well. Because he has work he sends money to me and my brother."*

- (When she left): *"sad, alone, without support";* (now): *"happy, content, supported with the money sent to take care of needs and situations that arise."*

These youth were not worried about the immediate present, whether or not they will have enough to eat today or a place to stay tomorrow. The sense of security and stability extended to their future, as many felt comfortable planning further study and career development with the continued financial support of their parent(s).

The sense of well being was not universal. In four of the situations, the youth indicated that they felt abandoned emotionally. Several mentioned that they had no one who supported them emotionally. One states, "Now, I don't have emotional support from anyone. With my mother, we don't really talk because it is night time when she calls and this is just to give me a PIN number for the money she's sending, asking about things around the house, about how my brothers are doing." Another youth, who has struggled in school, remarked that "if she were here, I would have made choices in my life—more control, better study habits, more discipline."

Even in cases where there is frequent contact between the parents and children, the lack of day-to-day contact has taken a toll on the relationships. A number of the youth, who were content living with their grandparents, expressed these emotions:

- *"I feel that my grandparents—I love them like they are my real parents. They have always been around and almost never have I seen my parents.*

- *"I always have my parents but here I feel like I am surrounded by caring from my grandparents and my cousin. We are a complete family."*

- *"My parents always help me, and they love me, but the love I get is from my grandparents, and I love them. They are always beside me, through the good and the bad."*

- *"I get emotional help from my parents through our (phone) conversations, but the hugs and the caring come from my grandparents. Although my parents are caring, it is not the same."*

The *One Family, Two Countries* study did not capture the experience of the mothers who were separated from the children, but other studies of transnational families and contact with the parents in the United States speak to the sadness of the separation and the realization of the parents that their children are more connected to grandparents and other family members than they are to them.

In Joanna Dreby's 2009 study of Mexican mothers working apart from their children, the mothers said they initially felt comfortable when their children were left with their grandmothers. They would notice that the children would start calling grandmothers "mami" or "mama." That was acceptable until the child stopped referring to them as mother. Sonia Nazario is the author of the award-winning book *Enrique's Journey*, about a Honduran youth who after many attempts finally succeeds in reuniting with his mother living in the United States. In speaking about transnational families, Nazario said: "I have talked to hundreds of women from Central America and Mexico who have left children behind because they felt that it was the only way to support their family, and there is so much sadness for them in being apart."

In the *One Family, Two Countries* study, the youth were asked how they would feel if their parents were to return, and what would change in their lifestyle if this were to happen. It was clear from the responses that the return of the parents would be a mixed blessing. A number of the youth, such as this one, remarked on the advantages of having the parents back: "I would be happy and content to have them here to be able to do things together." In 70% of the situations, however, the youth commented on how their economic situation would change for the worse—the food that they ate, the clothing they wore, and other household factors. Many said that they would have to quit studying or work at the same time they went to school. The conflicted feelings about their parents' return is captured in these two comments:

- *"I would feel a little better because I would have someone to talk with about my problems, and now I am not able to talk with her. There would be a big difference—we could not have what we have now."*

- *"It would not be the same because I would have to work and study—it would be harder, personally. It would be strange because it's been a long time since I lived with him and I don't know how it would be. But I would feel very happy because he was close."*

The final function of the family, according to Benokraitis, is social class placement. As shown in the chapter "Economic Realities," there can be economic advantages for youth from the lower rungs of the economic ladder receiving remittances from parents working abroad. However, low-income youth whose parents live either in El Salvador or abroad are in many ways disadvantaged compared to middle- and upper-middle class Salvadoran youth. As described in the chapter "Education," aspirations for their children's education are strong for most Salvadorans, and the possibility of greater education for children is one impetus for parents to migrate. While remittances can provide the support for children to stay in school, with the hope that this will lead to a middle-class life, the parents do not have the social capital, the connections, or the lived experience of being middle-class that would aid their children in the journey to the middle class.

The functions of families that family scholar Nijole Benokraitis identified do not include protection of children/keeping children safe. That omission may come from the author's context of families and parenting in the United States. However, the safety of one's children is a preoccupation of the parents in El Salvador with whom I have spoken.

To understand the impact on parenting in a country with this much violence, researchers Rojas-Flores et al. have conducted focus groups with parents in urban areas with high degrees of criminal activity in the states/departments of La Libertad and San Salvador (San Salvador is a department as well as the largest city in the department and country). The goal was to determine the impact of having been exposed to or having experienced violence during the parents' early lives (for many, during the war) and at present on these adults' ability to parent and on their parenting styles. Participants included 36 parents, 30 of whom were 30 years of age or older. Participants filled out a survey where they reported both indirect and direct violence exposure. This survey lumped together experiences during the civil war and since then, with 57% reporting having been somewhere where someone was killed or hurt, and 72% reporting seeing at least one dead body in their community.

Parents talked about how the current level of violence in their communities affects their daily lives and consequently how they parent. They spoke of constant hypervigilance (being constantly "on guard") and chronic anxiety, not knowing what will happen next. Parents talked about not being sure that they would come home after a day's work, and unsure about their children's safety on a given day.

The anxiety and the constraints on daily living caused by gangs—not wanting or being able to go through streets controlled by gangs—leads to a weakened self-efficacy, in that half the parents voiced that they felt that they could not adequately protect their children. They also stated that their fears were affecting their parenting: being overprotective, teaching their children not to trust others. One parent said, "Now, the more we can protect our children, the better. If (*the child*) doesn't leave the house, better. If he doesn't get invited to a friend's house, better. And this is the way we act now, because we don't know what else to do."

Parents also spoke in those focus groups about positive adaptive parenting practices that they have adopted as a result of the situation in which they were living. These included spiritual and religious practices, healthy monitoring of children's activities and teaching about right and wrong, and an overall increased value for family life. Some participants spoke about how they were finding or making meaning in the midst of current adversities, how they were spending more time in family activities, and how they were working hard on having good communication with their children.

How do families and family structures both support and limit youth?

There are clear positives for youth who have one or more parents working abroad who send home remittances—a better standard of living, more access to continuing education, and in some cases, more freedom. Disadvantages of the transnational family include the loss of contact between parent and child and the sorrow that comes with this—especially as felt by the child.

For many Salvadoran youth, good communication within their family is a strong source of support. In the national survey by Ramos, youth 15–29 years old were asked, "Who do you confide in most to talk about your problems?" Slightly over half (50.3%) of both males and females said that it was their parents. The next most common responses were significant others (17.5% for males, 21.4% for females) and friends (6.9% for both males and females).

When my co-researcher Virginia Quintana and I conducted focus groups in 2008 with high school students from Nombre de Jesus and Hacienda Vieja, we found similar results. We posed a scenario—"A friend, someone you can trust, comes to you and says that there is a *coyote* (smuggler) who is going to come the next day to take the friend to the U.S. A relative living there is paying for it, and you can come along without cost." The youths in the focus group were asked to indicate whom they would talk with about the decision whether to go or stay.

The youths came from an area where migration is common. They had recounted to us stories of people they knew who had tried to get to the U.S. and had come back without reaching their goals, and in one case had gone missing. If they were offered an essentially free and risk-free passage to the United States, 34 of the 36 youth stated that their parents would be the most important persons they would talk with in making that decision.

That adolescents actually talked to their parents was a significant change from what I had observed when I lived in El Salvador in the early 1970s. My view of how teens and their parents talked with each other in the poor community where I lived seemed fairly similar to what I was used to growing up in East Tennessee. In both cases, there was what I would call traditional parent-child communication—parents told children what to do, and children either obeyed or found passive-aggressive ways to get around them. Physical forms of enforcing rules were used. Thinking back on my teen years, there must have been members of my generation who talked frequently to their parents when they were not required to and confided in them; I just did not know any of them. If they did, it was not something that you would mention to friends. Plus, when I got to college in the mid-1960s, if you wanted to talk to someone on the telephone, you went to a pay phone and called home collect; you did not call home much.

In the United States, how teens and emerging adults relate to their parents has markedly changed. A recent study—Levine and Dean's (2012) *Generation on a Tightrope: A Portrait of Today's College Student*—found that about 40% of college students today are in contact with parents at least once a day by phone, email, text, or personal visit. The change in communication patterns has been helped not only by the ease of technology but also by a change in relationships between children and parents. According to Jon Gould, an American University professor and author of *How to Succeed in College (While Really Trying)*: "One thing that's different about the generation of parents and kids today is that they grew up for the most part liking one another. ... And that's different than ... the baby boomers that grew up rebelling against their parents."

Since 2005 in El Salvador, I had heard from teens in focus groups we conducted and from other youth that parent-child interactions were positive. The survey results quoted earlier in this chapter corroborated this, as did Santacruz Giralt and Carranza's

2009 national survey of youth aged 15–24, in which 82.8% of the youth said they were very satisfied with the quality of the relations within their family.

To understand family communication from someone who both studies and teaches about Salvadoran families, I met with Dr. Candelaria Navas, who has taught sociology at the National University for over two decades. When I asked how families have changed and what factors influenced that, her response was this:

> *How the family has improved—much of that is due to how the women's movement has influenced our society. Women begin to see themselves differently, and then they see the family differently. This also has affected relationships within couples. There has been a cultural shift in that now it is okay for couples, for youth, to talk about emotions. An example of this, which you would not have seen before, was a letter in 1996 from a youth whose father had died. In the letter, the young man said that he was sorry that he had never hugged his father.*

> *[W]hen I first taught a class on family in 1998, there were 8 men and 10 women in the course. During all that semester the males never talked in class. Now, the males are active participants in the class, and yes, they talk with their parents far more openly than did Salvadorans in the past.*

Being connected to one's family goes beyond good communication. There is a sense of obligation, of bending your own life decisions to the needs and well being of the family, that I do not see much among young adults in the United States. In our research in Chalatenango, Virginia Quintana and I found that for youth, the decision to migrate was often a family decision. A *coyote* would be paid and a young man sent North because the family needed the support. I have often found, in conversations with Salvadorans who have siblings working in the United States, that the reason that this person stayed was that one of the adult children needed to be in El Salvador to take care of the parent or parents. We also found this sense of family obligation in our 2011 study *Migration and Life Plans of Young Women in El Salvador*, conducted in Hacienda Vieja and Nombre de Jesús. In that study, we interviewed 18 young women who had graduated from high school in 2009 and 2010 about their current activities and future plans. At least 20% stated that they were not pursuing higher education or jobs outside the area because there was a need for them to be in the home.

In these cases, the relations that the youth and young adults had with their families fit with the observation of researchers Reed Larson and Suzanne Wilson that, in non-individualistic societies like those characteristic of Latin America, youth seek not emotional independence from their parents, but interdependence.

From the results of *Migration and Life Plans of Young Women in El Salvador*, it also appears that while young women's educational achievements equal or surpass their male counterparts, there has been little or no change in the division of household responsibilities in recent decades. We asked these young women how the work of the household—the care of children, the preparation of food, washing clothes, and house cleaning—was divided up. Their families typically had a piece of land where corn, beans, and vegetables were grown. When we asked the young women who did how many tasks around the house, the responses were: the daughters—36, the mother—23, the husband—6, and a few for other female relatives living in the house (e.g. niece, daughter-in-law, aunt). The socialization that household work is women's work appears to start from childhood, and the care of children and anything within the house is seen as the province of women. The men and male children worked the land, except in cases where the husband and male children had emigrated.

For all the challenges that Salvadoran families face—separation by distance, parents' splitting up, economic woes, the presence of violence—it is clear that youth in general find family to be a major source of support. For women, this can become a source of tension when they opt not to follow traditional roles, when the desire to follow one's own path conflicts with parental wishes and strong familial obligation. This connection with family, shown in survey results and in our own research, appears to contribute to Salvadorans' high ranking worldwide as to degree of well-being and happiness. This fits with published research on happiness, in which relationships with family and friends seem to predict positive feelings, and that social and personal trust in one's family leads to greater happiness.

6

Migration

It's hard to overstate the impact that migration has had on El Salvador over the past 40 years. Youth and adults have been leaving El Salvador in large numbers since the years of the civil war. Now, a third of Salvadorans have migrated and live elsewhere, mostly in the United States. Mexico is the only country with a greater number of its people living in the United States than El Salvador.

Aspects of migration as they relate to family have been discussed in the last chapter. In this chapter I will compare migration in El Salvador to that of other countries, and examine the ways that Salvadorans both in the U.S. and in their home country live transnational lives. Using the concept of supporting and hindering forces, I will show how migration supports Salvadoran youth and their families and how both the dangers of migrating and the fixation on leaving negatively affect youth.

A 2005 report by the United Nations Development Program (UNDP) described El Salvador as a country with transnational features, but that characterization sounds too abstract to me; it does not communicate the magnitude of the impact of migration on the country.

Start by considering the prevalence of migration in El Salvador compared with other countries. Geographer Harm de Blij argues that most of the 7 billion people on this earth will live and die close to where they were born:

> In their lifetimes, [this] vast majority will have worn the garb, spoken the language, professed the faith, shared the health conditions, absorbed the education, acquired the attitudes, and inherited the legacy that constitutes the power of place: the accumulated geography whose formative imprint still dominates the planet.

Most people stay, if not close to home, at least within the country in which they were born. Only 3% of the world's population are international migrants. For those born in the United States, the figure is much lower. The United States State Department estimates that there are 5 million to 5.5 million Americans living overseas— that's 0.2%. When I went to El Salvador in 2005, I was told that the country had a population of slightly over 7 million. When the every-10-years census was conducted in 2007, it was discovered that the country's population was only 5.7 million; the number of people who had left the country was far greater than had been estimated.

The reasons for people to leave El Salvador—indeed to leave any country—are often categorized in terms of push and pull factors, which either impel people to leave or attract them to move somewhere else. Push factors can include a lack of jobs or opportunities in your country; a repressive, authoritarian, and/or corrupt government; war or political unrest; lack of security; and natural disasters. In the latter part of the chapter, these will be discussed related to forces that specifically support or hinder youth coming of age.

Aside from push and pull, there is a third factor driving migration for Salvadorans, other Central Americans, and Mexicans. Of the people born in Mexico, 11% now live in the United States, and for El Salvador the figure is much higher. The extent of migration from El Salvador means that, in the words of migration researcher Suzanne Kent, "transnational migration has become an embedded sociocultural feature of El Salvador."

But the large number of Salvadorans in the U.S. means that in many places in the United States, too, there are social networks of family members and others from the same town or city who connect immigrants to jobs and housing in a structure of social capital.

Social capital refers to social relations that have productive results, to information, and to other valuable things that come from one's social networks—those family members, friends, and acquaintances with whom we interact. Douglas Massey and his colleagues apply this concept to migration, stating that "each act of migration alters the social context within which subsequent migration decisions are made, thus increasing the likelihood of additional movement. Once the number of network connections in a community reaches a critical threshold, migration becomes self-perpetuating." An example of recreating one's community in another country comes from Hacienda Vieja, which has 120 families; there is a soccer team in Northern Virginia that carries the name of the community, composed almost entirely of men from that community. These less-recent immigrants also serve as cultural brokers, providing information on how to relate to public authorities.

In *The Power of Place,* de Blij makes the distinctions between "Locals," individuals whose plans and actions keep them in their community and country of origin, and "Mobals," the "risk-takers, migrants willing to leave the familiar, to take a chance on new and different surroundings, their actions ranging from legal migration to undocumented border crossing, their motivations from employment to asylum." I read de Blij's quote about "taking a chance on new and different surroundings" and I am not sure that the surroundings in parts of the United States would be as new and different for Salvadorans as they would be to immigrants from countries with less migration. There are 800,000 Salvadorans in Los Angeles; half a million in Washington, DC and the Northern Virginia area; 225,000 on Long Island in New York; 2,600 in Little Rock, Arkansas; 15,000 in Salt Lake City, etc. If one leaves El Salvador, undocumented, for San Francisco, where one's brother lives, it is very possible that the brother lives in the Mission District, a neighborhood with a high number of Salvadorans and other Central Americans. For this new immigrant, there is much that is new and different—language and customs—and the uncertainty about being able to stay; however, there may also be many parts of the day-to-day living that are familiar.

The extent to which going (or trying to get) to the United States is an accepted part of life was apparent when I interviewed a teacher in Huertas, a small community 10 miles from the city of Ilobasco. The teacher said that when students finished 5th grade, they could go 7 miles to a middle school, or to Ilobasco, "but most of them, they don't continue. They stop studying, because they know that when they get to be 18 or earlier, they will leave (the country)."

These youth may leave the country, but the government of El Salvador has been very purposeful in efforts to stay connected with Salvadorans who have migrated and encouraged these migrants to stay connected to their country. In 2004, the government created a Vice-Ministry for El Salvadorans Living Abroad within the Ministry of Foreign Affairs. This ministry provides legal services to migrants, provides information on remittance services, encourages Salvadorans living abroad to connect with hometown associations, and even provides legal advice on how to buy property in El Salvador when one is away. Salvadorans who become citizens of other countries are allowed to maintain their El Salvador citizenship. Perhaps the most significant action for strengthening ties with those living abroad was the legislation that allowed Salvadorans living in the U.S. to vote in the 2014 Salvadoran presidential elections.

Migration engenders migration, and it also leads to what Levitt and Schiller have described as "conceptualizing simultaneity":

> Transnational migrants work, pray, and express their political interests in several contexts rather than in a single nation-state. Some will put down roots in a host country, maintain strong homeland ties, and belong to religious and political movements that span the globe. These allegiances are not antithetical to one another.

Think of a 34-year-old Salvadoran who left El Salvador 8 years ago to find work and support her children. She now lives and works in Houston, where she shares an apartment with three other women. One is her cousin. There is a computer in the apartment, and before she goes to work she Facebooks with her daughters, who live in the small city of Santa Rosa de Lima in the eastern part of the country. During the day she is speaking English as she interacts with her co-workers, most of them born in the United States. After work, she may go to one of the forty Salvadoran restaurants in Houston (there are 150,000 Salvadorans in Houston). She may also call her daughters in El Salvador or talk with a sister who lives in Los Angeles. Her daily life is a simultaneous one, in that her daily activities and routines are located both in the United States and El Salvador.

Living in El Salvador, it is not only the lives of one's relatives in the United States but the United States itself that is important in people's lives. An example of this comes from one of the two largest newspapers: the *Prensa Gráfica* has a section on goings-on in the department (state) of San Salvador, a section on events in the other 13 departments, and then a page on Department Fifteen—the United States. Obviously, Salvadorans don't think of the U.S. as their country's 15th state, but the term captures the connectedness of the two countries. (As a historical footnote, after independence from Spain in 1822, El Salvador did petition for inclusion in the United States.) In March 2013, when I called San Salvador to talk with my co-researcher Virginia Quintana, she asked me what I thought of the primary in the mayor's race in Los Angeles. Living 2,000 miles from Los Angeles, I knew that Mayor Antonio Villaraigosa was not running again, but was not following the race. In El Salvador, given that more than three-quarters of a million Salvadorans live in Los Angeles, the mayor's race was significant.

When we examine how migration affects youth as they move from adolescence to adulthood through the framework or lens of forces that support and forces that limit or harm youth, major forces that support youth are remittances while they are in El Salvador, and the potential benefits for them of migrating. Connected to this is the hindering force of the dangers of migration and, for those emigrating without authorization, the difficulties of working and living in the United States when one is undocumented.

In a national survey by Ramos, 38.4% of the responding youth cited lack of work as a reason people leave their country of origin. One can thus think of the lack of jobs as a push factor. Conversely, the prospect of work or economic opportunities elsewhere would be a pull factor. Migration to the United States for better opportunities is a universal phenomenon, and even more common in countries where it is difficult to find work. Even when the jobs that immigrants can find are in the so-called 3D jobs—dirty, difficult, and dangerous—in comparison with the prospects in one's own country there can be an enormous opportunity differential.

Thinking about migration in terms of opportunities to help oneself and one's family is cogently framed in the United Nations Development Program's 2005 publication *A Look at the New Us: The Impact of Migrations:*

> *Migration can [also] be seen as a resource for people, who decide to run all those risks in order to clear themselves a path towards human development. Families and communities adopting this strategy usually get access to opportunities they lacked back home. Through hard work and sacrifice, many migrants become well-off, and, with others who are still in a difficult situation, send support to their loved ones and to a lesser degree to their communities, thus contributing to reduce poverty levels and improve human development.*
>
> ...
>
> *In that sense, migration has encouraged autonomous solutions to problems of poverty and lack of human development. Without waiting for official programs, migrants have succeeded in making development happen for themselves and for their families, by investing human social capital, i.e., their own wits, work, and sacrifices, with the support of social networks. Their children, who still live in El Salvador, achieve higher education, live in better houses, and if the prospects in the country are not bright enough, they can always follow their parents' example.*

It is not just that there are not sufficient work opportunities per se, but that many Salvadorans see more opportunities for themselves and for their families elsewhere—or in the words of the report cited above, they are pursuing "autonomous solutions to human development," taking the initiative to make life better. This sentiment was expressed in Ramos's study of youth in which, while almost 40% of the youth stated that a reason for leaving your own country was the lack of work, a greater number, 50.9%, said that people emigrate because "they want to get ahead."

When I asked Pedro Barreras, one of those profiled in the "Stories" chapter, if he planned to go back to El Salvador, to go back to his community, he replied, "There are so many opportunities here." That drive to get ahead seems to be representative of many Salvadorans. Referring to their initiative, I have heard it said that "Salvadorans are the New Yorkers of Latin America," and an anthropologist who had studied Salvadoran immigrants on Long Island, New York, said that he heard a common theme from them: "We work harder than Americans."

Supporting the families is one major reason that Salvadorans migrate. For example, Pedro Barreras sends money back to his mother in Chalatenango. When we conducted a focus group with youth in 2010 in a community not far from where Pedro had lived, we found that none of the young men planned to move permanently to the United States—all but one wanted to be farming or raising cattle. However, all of these indicated that they would be working in the United States within 5 years, as this was the only way to save up enough money to buy land.

While migration to the United States can be seen as a positive for many youth, there are immense dangers inherent in unauthorized migration that constitute a hindering force. Many youth try multiple times to make the long trek from El Salvador to the United States. They are turned back in Guatemala or Mexico or perhaps make it to the United States border. The risk of the trip has also been normalized for many who see the risk as the price for making it to *El Norte*. And the risk is very real. According to Amnesty International's Annual Report on Mexico, 2012,

> *Tens of thousands of mainly Central American irregular migrants travelling to the USA were at risk of kidnapping, rape, forced recruitment or being killed by criminal gangs, often operating in collusion of public officials. Those responsible were almost never held to account. In February, the CNDH reported that 11,000 migrants had been kidnapped over a six-month period.*

Death counts are also high, though as the same report states, "inadequate methods of collecting and preserving evidence [hamper] identifications." The Committee of Relatives of Dead and Missing Migrants of El Salvador (COFAMIDE) says that 319 Salvadorans have disappeared in Mexico since 2006.

Unable to afford other means of transportation and wanting to avoid Mexican immigration checkpoints, thousands of Salvadorans and other Central Americans hop on top of moving freight trains going from southern Mexico to many northern destinations along the U.S.-Mexican border. In 2009, a Salvadoran consul in Mexico estimated that 20,000 persons had boarded the train in the first 9 months of the year. Riding the "Train of Death" or "The Beast," as it is called, is incredibly dangerous. Human rights groups estimate that thousands of migrants have died after falling off the train, due to fatigue, dehydration or attempts to board while it was on the move. Thousands more have fallen under the wheels and lost legs or arms—and in some cases both.

On top of the train, there is also danger from predators. Sonia Nazario is a *Los Angeles Times* reporter who won two Pulitzer prizes for a series of articles on the danger of undocumented migration from Central America to the United States. She subsequently wrote a highly recommended book on this subject: *Enrique's Journey*. In an interview, she describes her experience riding on the top of Mexican trains in order to experience what it was like for migrants:

> *I felt in constant danger and constantly looking out for people who could hurt me. In Chiapas, in southern Mexico, even when riding with six armed members of this immigration rights group, and they had AK-47s and shotguns, there were gangsters on top of the trains who were still robbing people at knife point at the back end of my train. The danger was always very real, when you would have gangsters lurking around the train stations with machetes. Another day I was interviewing people along a river in Oaxaca, southern Mexico, and I interviewed a girl who described being raped in the exact spot I had been in a day earlier.*

The dangers of migrating do not stop when one makes it across the border. In 2012, a pregnant Salvadoran was held captive when captured by criminals who preyed on migrants on the Texas side of the border. "They were threatening me with a gun, pointed right to my stomach," Zoila Figueroa said. She was freed after her husband, who lives on Long Island, New York, paid $3990 in ransom.

Not all undocumented travel to the United States comes with such risk. Some *coyotes*, or smugglers, who are paid to take immigrants across borders, will abandon them or sell them to narco-traffickers, but I have also heard that there are coyotes who are both trustworthy and effective. In Hacienda Vieja, I was told that all who attempt the journey using the same *coyote* get across on the first try.

Once immigrants get to the United States, there is the risk of deportation. Under the Obama administrations, the number of those deported has increased, and approximately 400,000 undocumented immigrants are deported each year. The increased risk of deportation has caused many undocumented immigrants to "live in the shadows" even more, only leaving their houses to go to work or to very necessary places.

Outside of the framework of supporting and hindering forces, the scarcity of jobs and the reality that migration has become so common affects the ways that young Salvadorans think about their future. José William Garcia, a social worker who worked with youth and ex-gang members in Ilobasco, has told me, "For youth, going to the United States—it is the only horizon they see, the only horizon."

In the opening pages of the chapter, I contrasted the high percentage of Salvadorans living outside their country with the situation in the United States. As I talk to Salvadorans about migration, in addition to the asking if they have thought of going to the United States, I often ask: "Why do you stay here?" On the surface it's a strange question to be asking—"Why stay in your home country, your own country?" I ask that in talking with youth, in focus groups, to taxi drivers, in conversation with Salvadorans that I know or meet.

In 2012, I asked a group of first-year college students at the University of Wisconsin-Whitewater, "Why do you plan to stay in the United States?" There was a pause before answering this question; it was not a question that they expected. When these young adults think about their future, they do not think of leaving their country. They may think of moving to a larger city in the Midwest, like Minneapolis or Chicago, or someplace warmer like Florida or Arizona, but not out of the country. In El Salvador, people answer that question quickly. In Ramos's national survey on youth, about half responded that they have thought about going to the U.S. The older the youth, the more that they think about leaving—heading north, hoping to be a stranger in a strange land, but with more economic prospects than they see at home.

As Princeton sociologist Alejandro Portes explains, both the reality of a transnational society created by migration and the prospect of migration affects youth greatly. If they happen to be a member of a family where someone has migrated and sends back remittances, the chance for getting an education and an improved quality of life is greater. Also, when the prospects for employment and advancement are limited, migrating can be an autonomous solution to human development. However, the impact of the restricted range of choices that many Salvadorans perceive—stay and try to find low-wage work or emigrate—is that many youth become focused on out-migration, neglecting their education and the search for occupational opportunities in their own society.

7

Education

Depending on the lens one uses in looking at education in El Salvador, one can either marvel at how far the country has come in educating its citizenry in a relatively short period of time or despair at how Salvadoran education matches up with what is needed for the 21st century.

In this chapter I will use an example to illustrate the limited range of opportunities, especially in rural areas, that many Salvadorans faced in getting an education not that many decades ago. I will look briefly at the history of education in El Salvador, the challenges that the country has faced in increasing access and quality, and the how the education system supports and limits young Salvadorans today.

When I was teaching at the Universidad Panamericana in 2005, one of my students was Andrés Dominguez, a community health promoter for the Salvadoran Ministry of Health who was pursuing his social work degree part-time. Andrés's story is not typical, and neither is he, but it does illustrate how opportunities in El Salvador have changed. Here is his account of his educational journey:

> I am from Cantón Huertas, a group of houses 16 kilometers (*about ten miles*) from the city of Ilobasco. When I was

young, we had to go to Ilobasco on foot and on horseback. It was all small farmers at that point. In my family, there were my mother and father and nine children; six of us live in El Salvador now.

In the community, there was one school with one teacher, with only 1st and 2nd grades. When I started school, in 1976, from my house it was three and a half kilometers to get to school. So I would start school each year, but when it got to growing season, we were too busy in the fields for me to go to school. So I never completed a grade, and after the age of 9, did not attempt going. There was only one teacher, and many weeks she would have a meeting in Ilobasco. On foot or on horseback, she would take off a day to get there, a day for the meeting, a day to come back. My father did not see any use for us to walk to school only to see it closed so many days; it was better that I stay home and work. There was always work in the fields, and little money; I walked around barefoot until I was 12 years old.

But ever since I was little, I had wanted to learn. I wanted to be a professional. I don't remember a time when I did not want to be a professional.

When my oldest brother was 16, he left to go to the United States to work. While traveling through Mexico, he met a Salvadoran living there. They got along really well. The man was middle-aged, without kids, and told my brother that if he came back to El Salvador, my brother could live with him and his wife in Santa Tecla, close to San Salvador. My brother told him that no, he was going to the United States, but that he had a younger brother (*Andrés*), who really wanted to go to study, to go to school, but there were not schools in the community and the family did not have the money to send him off to study. When this man came back to El Salvador, he sought me out, and asked if I wanted to come and live with them. I could help take care of his mother and go to school.

So when my parents gave me permission, I moved to Santa Tecla and started 1st grade. I was 15 years old then, in a class with 6-year-olds. That was in 1986. At first I did not want to actually go to school because of the age difference. They had to find a special desk big enough for me. But I did go, and I stayed there through 4th grade. Then, when this gentleman went back to Mexico, I moved back in with my family in Huertas.

I continued studying in a program on Saturday and Sunday in Ilobasco. I would have to leave by 4 a.m. to walk to get to class by 8 a.m. I completed 5th and 6th grade that way. When I finished 6th grade, in 1992, an official from the Health Ministry came to my community looking for people who wanted to be health promoters in their home community. At that time, you only had to have a 6th-grade education. I applied and was hired.

So I worked as a health promoter in Huertas and the neighboring communities during the week, and kept getting up early on Saturdays and Sundays to attend school in Ilobasco, and finished 9th grade there. Afterwards, thanks to a Chilean non-governmental organization, I was able to get my high school degree part-time while I continued to work. When I finished in 1997, I wanted to go on to college, but there were no programs where I could attend school and keep working.

In 2000 I was one of four Salvadoran health promoters selected to go to the United States for a 6-month training on community health practice at a community college in El Paso, Texas. This education motivated me to look again at going to college. Another health promoter told me that he was studying social work at the Universidad Panamericana in San Salvador, with classes mostly on weekends, with only a few classes at night during the week. This fit my schedule, and I had gotten to know social workers during my training in El Paso, so I applied, was accepted, and started classes in 2004. So that's what I did, went on nights and weekends over 5 years, and graduated in November 2009.

Two months before I graduated, I was called in to the regional health office in San Vicente, and offered this position,

Regional Technical Coordinator, in charge of all the health promotion and health promoters in three departments (states). This was three positions or levels above where I had been. The week after getting my college diploma, when I met the education requirements, I was formally offered the position and I accepted it.

Andrés's account shows the lack of educational opportunities for Salvadorans in rural areas several decades ago, and that was a continuation of a historical trend. Going back to the 1800s, both under colonial rule and then independence, education was not a priority of the government. There were few schools, almost all of them in urban areas. Teacher training was rare, and often older students were used to teach younger ones. Compulsory public education was not mandated until 1885, but this was only for boys ages 7 to 15. Education for girls was at the discretion of the parents, and boys who lived more than a mile from a school were not required to go to school.

During the first half of the 20th century there was an increase in the training of teachers and the government constructed some schools, but by mid-century the number of children in school was still minimal. In 1950, between 40 and 50% of the population was illiterate, and in 1951 only one half of school-age children were enrolled in school. Most who went to school stopped after the 2nd grade; only 1 in 18 students was in high school.

During the civil war that lasted from 1978–1992, education became much less of a priority for the government and schools in many rural areas closed. At the end of the war, 40% of the population in rural areas had completed no more than 1 year of school, only 14% had a 6th-grade education, and only 1% had a high school education.

Over the past 20 years and especially the last decade, the number of schools and the number of students in schools has greatly increased. Speaking about the community where he grew up, Andrés Dominguez documented the rise in availability of schooling since he was a child there:

By 1994 we had two more schools in my community, one that went up to 5th grade. Now, we have 7 schools, one that goes through 9th grade, and there are a total of 35 teachers in the schools.

We had to work to get those schools. Groups were organized in the very small communities and we would go to the Ministry of Education to ask for the schools. We went so often with the message "We need a school in this community" that I think the officials got tired of us and gave in. What would happen is that the Ministry would supply the materials, the community would then build the school, and the Ministry would then provide the teachers.

Still, this is one of the most mountainous and inaccessible parts of El Salvador, and there still are places where children have to walk 5 or 6 kilometers to get to school.

Starting from the mid-1990s, governments have made concerted efforts to increase access to school, to improve the quality of the teaching, and to use schools to bring more cohesion to the country and strengthen the sense of national identity.

When Mauricio Funes and the FMLN gained the presidency of El Salvador in 2009, one of his priorities was to make education more inclusive. The most visible aspect of the education reform has been the provision of supplies for all public school students. In El Salvador, while public education is free, parents had been responsible for providing uniforms (worn in all public and most private schools), shoes, and school supplies. The cost of these had kept some low-income children out of school. Shortly after winning the election, the new government announced that they would be providing two sets of uniforms, a pair of shoes, and school supplies to more than 1.3 million pupils.

One initiative of the Funes administration to improve the quality of education that has received broad support is the Inclusive Full-Time Schools program. Students in public schools generally only go to school for 4 hours, in the morning or afternoon. This program reserves the half-day when students are not in school for enrichment activities, often with the help of community members and volunteers. However, the quality of this depends on the resources and infrastructure of the schools.

The Full-Time School initiative, along with a renewed emphasis on teaching illiterate adults to read, reflects the philosophy behind the government's *Plan Social Educativo* (PSE). The PSE has aimed to reform the education system "to develop citizens with critical judgment, able to reflect and investigate, and to construct collectively new knowledge that allows the transformation of social reality and values and protects the environment." This plan continues in the Sanchez Cerén presidency.

While the growth in the number of schools and the 93–95% attendance in primary schools is impressive, the question remains: what factors help and hinder young Salvadorans in getting an education, and how does getting an education help them move forward in their lives?

One of the factors responsible for increased school attendance and completion, from early grades through college, is remittances (see Appendix A for further information). Salvadorans working in the United States sent home 3.96 billion dollars in 2013; 22% of Salvadoran households receive remittances, most often between $150–$300 a month; and 91.6% of the families receiving remittances use the money for consumption, which includes education as well as housing costs and food.

One study by the National Bureau of Economic Research found that family income from remittances was a much stronger predictor of school attendance than other sources of family income. In urban areas, remittances have at least 10 times the effect of other income on not dropping out of school. In rural areas, the effect of remittances was 2.6 times that of other sources of income. The impact of remittances on the education of students suggests that those sending money from the United States, who also specify how the money is to be spent, may prioritize education.

But this prioritization differs according to life prospects. A World Bank study found that girls (11–17) and boys (11–14) from households that received remittances were more likely to stay in school than those from households that did not receive remittances. However, that positive effect does not carry over to boys 15 and older. A reason for this discrepancy may be that teen boys are much more likely, especially in some parts of the country, to emigrate than girls, and those who have already decided to leave may not see any reason for staying in school. Conversely, it may be the case that relatives in the U.S. may want to further the education of a late-adolescent girl because they want more for her than just marriage at a young age or caring for older relatives, and at the same time they know that job prospects are limited. They would prefer that this young woman be in school than at home and not doing anything, so they may direct remittances toward her further education.

Thanks to the above-mentioned cultural changes, the number of children who attend primary school is now close to 100%, but the dropout rate increases the older the students get. Only 60% of the children who start elementary school get to the 9th grade and still only 30% graduate with a high school degree. The quality of the education is also a concern. In 2013, El Salvador ranked 33rd out of 37 countries in the TIMSS test, which measures academic achievement in science and mathematics.

Reasons contributing to this are many. For one, there is insufficient funding. Education in El Salvador has never been well funded. Public spending on education remains low—between 2.8% and 3.6% of Gross Domestic Product (GDP) in 2008–2010. This is similar to its neighboring countries Honduras and Guatemala, but other countries in Latin America spend more—Costa Rica's education expenses are 10.5% of GDP, Argentina's are 9.5%, and Chile's are 8.2%. As one of the consequences, there are problems with the quality of the school facilities. For example, 48% of students go to schools without educational technology.

A second concern is that there are weaknesses in the initial and ongoing development of teachers. By way of illustration, a 2012 report states that 30% of teachers who work in schools with computers do not know how to use them in teaching. Luis Monterrosa, a school official at the Ministry of Education, told me that there are 40,000 teachers in the country. Some of them, according to Monterrosa, are as good as teachers in expensive private schools, and there are others, especially those over 50 who are "just there because they are too young to retire," who are used to the old ways of teaching where the teacher just lectures, and do not want to change. Some teachers are also resistant to the initiative of teaching students how to resolve conflicts, as this does not fit with the traditional curriculum.

The length of the school day creates a third problem for education quality in several respects. In order to educate more students without having to greatly increase the number of schools, educational reforms in 1995 shortened the school day to 4.5 hours and created two shifts in the school day—half the students would go to school in the morning, the other half in the afternoon. The shortening of the school day led to fewer hours of instructional time. A second problem comes with a number of teachers who teach both shifts for economic reasons, as teachers make between $400 and $700 a month. While a second shift is seen as necessary by teachers to support their families, it is not surprising to have a lack of teaching effectiveness toward the end of that 9-hour day. One teacher summed up the problem of teaching a double shift and the impact on teaching this way: "What you think is—the afternoons are wasted. But it is not that they are wasted, because the kids, they come to learn, but one is already tired. Me, I'm dragging (when they arrive)."

Despite the efforts and initiatives of recent governments, in far too many parts of the country schools just do not "work." I have heard complaints—similar to those that Andrés Dominguez explained in his story about his first attempts to go to school as a child in the 1970s—that teachers in rural schools will disappear for days at a time. The curriculum and teaching practices rely too little on involving students. In a country in which young people do not see the obvious payoff of education for jobs and there is the lure of emigrating without an education, the lack of quality is one more potent reason for adolescents to leave school.

Many Salvadorans who can afford it send their children to private schools. On the standardized tests given to all students, private school students scored almost 17% higher than students in public schools. I have been told that in San Salvador a pretty good private school costs about $100 a month per child. On the high end are the bilingual schools—the American School, the German School, the British School with an International Baccalaureate—which cost at least $3000–$4000 per student a year.

There are other determinants of a child's learning than school quality. The more educated the parents, the better they generally are in helping students with homework and helping them negotiate school. While the average number of years of schooling has increased since the end of the civil war, in 2012 it was only 8.3 years for the metropolitan San Salvador area, 7.7 years for all urban areas, and 3.6 years for the rural areas. The parents' lack of education (and in some cases literacy), combined with the absence of public libraries, leads to a culture where reading that is not required is not common. A Peace Corps Volunteer who lived and worked in a remote area of El Salvador was sitting on her front porch reading one day when and a couple of teenage girls approached her. They asked: "Are you taking a course?" "No, why." "Oh, we saw you reading, so we figured that you must be studying for a course." There is not a "culture of reading" within the schools or in the larger community in which students are both expected and encouraged to read.

The lack of reading both in the home and in pre-college schooling carries over when youth get to college. When I taught short courses to social work faculty at the University of Veracruz in Mexico 20 years ago, the teachers there complained about the lack of reading material and that their students were not used to reading. I found the same thing when I taught at the Universidad Panamericana in 2005—students there were overwhelmed by an amount of reading that would seem minimal in the United States (a book chapter or two a week). When I told the president of the Universidad Panamericana a couple of years ago that students in college in the United States read two or three books per course, he was astonished—and he has repeated that back to me several times since then: "Two or three books for every course?"

I was talking about the deficiencies in the primary–high school system and how they affect youth with Dr. Hector Samour, the Vice-Minister of Education in the Funes government and a former philosophy professor at the Universidad Centroamericana "José Simeon Cañas" (UCA). Dr. Samour said that at the UCA, students come in with such gaps in their education that they spend the first year trying to fill these, or there are a number of courses that they then have to repeat, and they get discouraged—they are spending money and time in class while not advancing very fast toward getting their degrees.

Another challenge for youth in getting an education lies in the high rate of adolescent childbearing. According to a United Nations Population Fund report in 2013, 1 in every 12 Salvadoran girls is a mother by the time she is 15; in the poorest areas of the country, that figure rises to 1 in 5. One of every three Salvadoran girls has had a baby by the time she is 18, and girls between the ages of 10 and 19 account for 29% of all births in the country.

El Salvador is not alone in having high teen pregnancy rates. El Salvador's historically high adolescent pregnancy rate is comparable to that of many Latin American countries. However, the number of children per woman has decreased by 60% in the last 30 years, from 6.3 lifetime births per woman in the mid-1970s to 2.5 by the late 2000s. Salvadoran adolescents and women in general, as in many other countries, are less likely to become pregnant if they are better off and have at least a high school education. The rate of contraception among wealthier Salvadoran women is 72%. While the rate of contraception among poorer women has increased by 20% in recent years, only 52% of the poorest Salvadoran women use contraceptives.

The demands of being a teen mother often interrupt other plans for Salvadoran youth. I was aware of this when I attempted to interview youth I had met with in 2005 for my documentary *Difficult Dreams*. In the very rural community of Huertas, near the small city of Ilobasco, lived Estela, a shy 13-year-old who excelled in school. She talked about how she would study in her spare time and wanted to be a teacher. Her parents, who were both living and working on Long Island, New York, were very willing to support her education. In 2012, I attempted to interview her again. I was not able to make contact, but I found that she was now living in Ilobasco, and at 20 years of age had two children. Estela's earlier dreams and present situation are a reminder that adolescent plans for the future can change.

Until recently, higher education in El Salvador was only for the few. When I went to El Salvador in 1970, the only higher education institutions were the Universidad de El Salvador—referred to as UES or the Nacional, with a main campus in San Salvador and branch campuses in the cities of Santa Ana and San Miguel—and the UCA.

Even before the civil war broke out, the UES had been a center for protest and anti-government activities. It was occupied in 1972 and 1973, and often during the course of the war; students could not count on uninterrupted semesters. Even in the times that the university was not occupied, students, professors, and university authorities were often the target of government forces and paramilitaries. In 1980, the Chancellor, Felix Ulloa, was assassinated. The UCA was founded in 1965, supported by prominent Salvadoran families who wanted an alternative to the Nacional (and another option for their children other than studying abroad). During the civil war, the UCA was the home of internationally recognized Jesuit intellectuals, many of whom were strong proponents of liberation theology.

In El Salvador, colleges and universities have been and are regulated by the national government, not independent accrediting organizations. With the government preoccupied by the war and the National University closed at times, there was essentially no oversight of higher education by the national government during the war years through the early 1990s. In that time, small universities, many of which were for-profit, opened without any legal authorization. Some of these had ill-defined programs and low standards for graduation. When the Higher Education Law was passed in 1995, tightening standards, 18 universities were closed. At present, there is the one National University, now with multiple branches, and 24 private universities (some nonprofit and some for-profit), as well as technical institutes.

College enrollment has grown over the past decades, and increased 20% between 2006 and 2010. Because of access issues in rural areas, most of that increase came in urban areas. In Ramos's national study on Salvadoran youth, he found that 21.9% of urban high school grads had either attended or were attending college, compared with 4.8% of those in rural areas.

My understanding of the rise in college enrollments is that this is partially due to the greater awareness of youth living in a connected age of possibilities outside the traditional ones of their parents and grandparents. Also, remittances from parents or relatives in the

United States have made higher education affordable for a growing number of Salvadorans. Because job opportunities are limited for those with a high school education, many young Salvadorans opt to continue their education.

Students go to college because they believe that they will acquire the learning and skills that will serve them well after graduation. However, just as in the preparatory grades, there are significant issues with quality and coherence in higher education in El Salvador.

While tuition is affordable at many of the universities ($40–$100 a month during the semesters), the low cost translates into poorly paid teachers with low levels of education themselves. For full-time teachers, the typical salaries are low, at $500–$1000 a month. In 2010, 21% of those teaching in college had Masters degrees, just 1.2% had Ph.Ds., and the rest only had a Bachelor's degree. The majority of the teachers are part-time, often making as little as $6 an hour for the classes they teach. Some of those, like a family court mediator I know, are working professionals who teach classes because they like educating about their field and having the contact with students. Others teach a number of courses at multiple institutions to get by, with little time for course preparation and reflection on their teaching.

The number of poorly educated and part-time instructors makes it harder for students to get the individualized attention that is often necessary for them to think beyond getting a degree and focus on acquiring the knowledge, skills, and experiences necessary for employment and success. A quote from a college teacher aptly illustrates this: "As a teacher, I am not preparing myself to see the qualities, see the potential, see the possibilities (in my students) …and then help the student to work with what he knows, his abilities, and based on this, come up with a productive solution. What we have does not work; we need to train the professors in new things."

According to higher education analyst Oscar Carlos Picardo, "higher education in El Salvador has opted in recent years for coverage over quality, and the result has been over-crowded classrooms, less money for research, and a style of teaching that does not go beyond the superficial. The students know the material but do not understand it, and they cannot apply what they have learned." Of the students who enter college in El Salvador, 90% do not graduate or do not graduate on time.

Large portions of those who leave do so for lack of funds to continue studying. However, the lack of job opportunities for those graduating and the fear that the degree may not be worthwhile are also major factors.

Data from the 2013 study by the United Nations Development Program showed that the economic payoff of graduating from college in El Salvador is limited, and this has continued to decline since 2000. One reason for that could lie in that the universities are graduating more students than there are available jobs, especially in business administration and law. Universities counter that the problem is with the highly centralized Ministry of Education, in which it is a very bureaucratic process to introduce new majors that might better suit the needs of the workplace.

Another reason is the perception among employers of the low quality of applicants. Marco Penado of Manpower El Salvador says that students are graduating without the technical skills and, for many positions, the necessary ability to speak English. An indication of this is that the call centers (for Dell and Sykes, for example) in El Salvador are largely staffed by Salvadorans deported from the United States). The perception of the lack of quality in the whole education system leads employers to raise education levels while not raising salaries. If employers cannot fit workers without a high school degree who have the skills they expect, they will hire high school graduates but pay them at the range for the non-high school grad. Similarly, college graduates may be hired for lower-paid positions instead of applicants with high school degrees.

Educators and government officials are aware of the deficiencies in elementary through high school and higher education and there are ongoing conversations about how to better prepare students so that they are competitive with students in other parts of the world. There are plans to update higher education, to increase the number of internships and real-world learning experiences for the students, and to better align the majors and careers of the students with available job openings and areas of need in the country. As Vice-Minister of Education Samour said in 2012: "We don't need more accountants (in the rural areas) in Morazán."

I read the critiques of higher education in El Salvador and agree with the criticisms. The curriculum is outdated and too inflexible, and the teaching methods are too traditional (with too little project-based and hands-on learning). However, I also am familiar with Salvadorans for whom higher education has been the catalyst that changed their lives.

First as a Fulbright Scholar in 2005 and since then through frequent visits, I have worked with the Universidad Panamericana de El Salvador and its entrepreneurial chancellor, Oscar Morán, and other faculty and staff there. The main campus in San Salvador and the branch campuses in the cities of San Vicente and Ahuachapán are not "high tech" by United States standards. This educational institution has perhaps the lowest tuition of the private universities. Like many other universities in El Salvador, there is an overreliance on part-time faculty members. Yet in these modest settings, I have seen futures transformed.

I think of students I know there who have graduated—the first in their family to attend and complete college—and went on to find jobs in the field of social work. I think especially of Denys Rodriguez, one of my students in 2005, who conducted interviews for one of our studies. In 2008, when he was buying a snack from a street vendor, a nearby security guard's automatic rifle accidentally went off, and a bullet pierced Denys' spinal column, causing paralysis. Denys did graduate from college, and after 3 years of applying, secured a position at a Ministry of Health facility working with disabled war veterans. Without the college degree, Denys would be stuck in a back bedroom of his mother's house.

I go back to the interviews in the "Stories" chapter with young adults for whom education has been important. None of the young adults in that chapter who have graduated from college in El Salvador—Douglas, Rebeca, and Luís, as well as Andrés whose account started this chapter—had parents who had gone to college or who had professional jobs. Douglas, the government auditor, acquired the knowledge and skills at the UCA to pass the tests to secure his position. Rebeca, now the Director of Administration and Finance at the Universidad Panamericana, told me about how valuable the courses in her business degree were in carrying out her job—especially the courses on finance and human resource management.

Also in the "Stories" chapter is the account of Maria Rosa, who was not able to attend college out of high school due to lack of funds, and now, married with children, is in college as a returning student. She reminds me of the returning students whom I teach at my university in Wisconsin—individuals who are aware of a tight job market, and yet see a college education as the only way to change the trajectory of what they do and accomplish in the world of work.

There is also the part of education not directly related to one's career, one's job. Both Luís and Douglas, studying at different universities, told me how important the philosophy classes were in their own development. And if El Salvador is to transcend the differences that have divided the country, the emphasis on citizenship that can come from education is crucial. The American Nobel Prize-winning economist Milton Friedman disapproved of much of what governments do, but supported government support of education, stating: "A stable and democratic society is impossible without a minimum degree of literacy and knowledge on the part of most citizens and without widespread acceptance of some common set of values. Education can contribute to both. In consequence, the gain from the education of a child accrues not only to the child or to his parents but also to other members of the society."

Yes, an education that is far more accessible than it was decades ago is making a difference in the lives of many Salvadorans. However, there are major steps that are needed to improve the quality of education from primary school through high school and into higher education. If El Salvador does this, that would open up many more opportunities both for individual young people and for the country.

8

Economic Realities

The economy of a country encompasses a number of distinct but related components. These include the economic system and the overall state of the economy and the economic well being of those living in that country. After examining these in El Salvador, this chapter will look at how economic factors affect the situation of Salvadoran youth coming of age as they enter the labor force.

Since the end of the civil war, El Salvador adopted and has maintained neoliberal economic policies. Neoliberal economic policies include selling off state-owned enterprises or utilities, cutting support for social programs and other government expenditures, lessening regulation of economic activities, and encouraging foreign as well as domestic private investment. Neoliberal economic policies also involve trade agreements that reduce tariffs that protect products and agricultural commodities in individual countries. Like the North American Free Trade Agreement (NAFTA), which involves the United States, Canada, and Mexico, there is a Central American Free Trade Agreement (CAFTA), which went into effect in 2006. El Salvador was the first country to sign.

After the Peace Agreements were signed in 1992 at the conclusion of the civil war, the conservative political party ARENA, which controlled the presidency and a majority in the legislature, reduced the government's investment in education and other government programs. The economy had a post-war boom from 1992 to 1995, with an annual economic growth of 6.8%. From 1996 to 2000, however, economic growth was reduced to 3.0% per year. The slowing of economic activities, along with the loss of government jobs and an increased demand for workers in the United States during the boom economic times of the late 1990s, led to more Salvadorans migrating to the United States without legal permission.

In 2001, the Salvadoran legislature effectively dollarized the economy—the U.S. dollar is the accepted currency in this country (as it is in Panama and Ecuador). As Clare Ribando Seelke explains, "dollarization led to lower interest rates, low inflation, and easier access to capital markets, but it also took away the government's ability to use monetary and exchange rate adjustments to cushion the economy from external shocks." The conversion from *colones,* the official currency, to dollars was also accompanied by a one-time rapid increase in prices.

In the years between 2000–2009, the economic growth in El Salvador was only 2.1% per year, less than in other Latin American countries. The 2008–2009 worldwide recession caused the Salvadoran economy to shrink by 3.1% in 2009, and the economy has not recovered. Hurricane Ida in late 2009 and Tropical Depression 12E in 2012 both caused damage to crops, infrastructure, and roads. The economy only grew 1.5% in 2011 and 1.3% in 2012. Economic growth is not projected to increase significantly for the next several years.

As part of an initiative from the government of the United States, the Partnership for Growth, a team of economists from the United States and El Salvador, did an extensive analysis of the constraints that appear to prevent the Salvadoran economy from growing. Some difficulties in the Salvadoran economy are related to changes in the world economy over the past decades. Foreign exchange is the term for the money that comes into a country through exports and other means. In 1978, 80% of the foreign exchange in El Salvador came from traditional agricultural exports: coffee, and to a smaller degree sugar cane and other crops. Other exports accounted for 8% of the foreign exchange, and remittances were another 8%. Maquilas—mainly textiles factories which import materials duty-free and then export the finished products—accounted for 2%

of the foreign exchange. By 2004, remittances had accounted for 70% of the foreign exchange, with traditional agriculture products only accounting for 5%. From year to year since then, depending on the coffee market, the extent of agriculture exports has varied, but does not get close to its past prominence.

Also prominent among the constraints on the Salvadoran economy is the cost of crime and violence, including losses due to theft and the cost of security. Carlos Acevedo, former director of El Salvador's Central Reserve Bank, estimated that the cost of violence in El Salvador was 10.8% of the Gross Domestic Product, higher than in other Central American countries. Of businesses surveyed in El Salvador, 47.8% identified crime as an obstacle to their operations; this was 15% higher than in other comparable countries.

As well as noting weakness in the Salvadoran manufacturing sector, the analysis on constraints on the economy showed that return on investments was lower than in other countries, with a smaller number of projects that can produce a desirable rate of return. This means that both Salvadorans and foreign investors wishing to maximize their investments could do better if they were to invest elsewhere.

Economically, El Salvador has changed dramatically since I lived in El Salvador in the early 1970s, when it was a predominantly rural country with an economy based on exporting coffee and sugar cane. The following description of one rural area four decades ago and now not only illustrates this but also shows how the work-related aspirations of youth have changed.

In 2009, my co-researcher Virginia Quintana and I wanted to understand how adolescents in an area of high migration envisioned their future. We carried out this project in a small town (Nombre de Jesus) and a much smaller community (Hacienda Vieja) in the mountainous northwest department (state) of Chalatenango. Nombre de Jesús and Hacienda Vieja are in the eastern part of the department, only miles away from Honduras. I had been to rural Chalatenango in the early 1970s, visiting John Scholefield, a Peace Corps Volunteer, who was serving in a community close to Nombre de Jesús. Working with community groups and with the support of a non-governmental organization, he assisted in getting safe drinking water to remote areas. I remember spending nights there in the countryside with John—in a house of adobe with a dirt floor. Without electricity, I realized in the night stillness that I was in a place where daylight meant activity and nighttime imposed rest. It was a place where these subsistence farmers were totally dependent on the rainy season to deliver neither too little nor too much rain.

The area has undergone changes since then. The first change came during the civil war. Chalatenango was one of the strongholds of the rebel forces fighting against the government, and the residents of many villages, including Hacienda Vieja, had to leave for resettlement camps in Honduras. After the war, the residents were able to come back home. However, in the mid-1990s when living costs were rising and jobs had not come to the region, migration to the United States greatly increased.

Going to Hacienda Vieja now, you encounter a different reality than I remember from the 1970s. Remittances that family members have sent from the United States over the years have paid for houses with stucco exteriors and tile floors. A student who was conducting research there in 2007 reported changes in the lifestyle of young people there due to the remittances: "Instead of refrescos (*traditional fruit drinks*), they only drink Coca-Cola. The way they dress—it's what they see on television."

Coming from San Salvador, where the sounds of traffic and city life do not cease, I was struck by the quiet and the slow pace of Hacienda Vieja. This does not mean that people are not active. When I first went there and heard the men talking about going and working in the fields in the morning, back by lunch, I had the idea of a 3- to 4-hour workday. In reality, many of the men are waking at 3:30 or 4:00 a.m., walking a ways to get out to the fields to start working in the grayness of early dawn. They may have worked 7 hours or more before leaving the fields to escape the hotter afternoon temperatures and return home for a late lunch.

The women are busy during the mornings, grinding corn, making tortillas from scratch, washing clothes by hand, and making and then carrying food out to the men working in the fields.

Afternoons are quieter. The men who have already done a day's work often take the traditional siesta. Some youth who go to school in the mornings are hanging around in shaded patios. There are card games, and some of the men are drinking beer. In the late afternoon, when it cools off, there are soccer or basketball games, these days with teams that cross gender and age differences.

The father of Thelma—whose account is in the chapter "Stories"—has worked as a health promoter, one of the few formal jobs in this community of 100 families. One woman has a small store and at least one person drives a pickup—passengers stand in the truck bed—to the small town of Nombre de Jesús and then to the city of Chalatenango. The pickup leaves at 8:00 in the morning. The trip takes two hours to get to Chalatenango, and the pickup heads back at 2:00 p.m. There is enough time to make purchases, or go to the bank to pick up remittances sent from family members in the United States, but not enough time to work a job.

In 2009, Ms. Quintana and I conducted two modified focus groups with youth who were in high school in Nombre de Jesús and Hacienda Vieja, as well as with youth aged 18–24 who were no longer in school—33 youths in total. We also met with community leaders. There were questions about family communication and migration, which are reported in other parts of the book. Additionally, we asked them to draw on a sheet of paper, using crayons, themselves as adults—how they envisioned their lives in terms of work, family, where they would live, etc.

On the next page is a sample of the drawings. Approximately a third of the participants were male, and the two drawings from young men are representative of all but two of the males. The males drew themselves with fields of corn or with livestock, and a number of them also showed themselves playing soccer.

In the case of the young women, they had at least one foot squarely placed in the 21st century. I asked my colleague Jo Ellen Burkholder, an anthropologist who has worked in Latin America, to analyze the drawings. She immediately noted the high heels, the styles of dresses, skirts, and blouses, which reflected what these young women were seeing on television. Only 1 of the 21 young women drew herself in the style of clothes that women traditionally wear in the countryside.

These female high school students drew themselves as adults with jobs in the formal economy, as doctors, nurses, schoolteachers, secretaries, accountants. Alongside images of their future selves, they drew pictures of where they would be living. Without

exception they drew pictures of houses in the country, almost always the only house shown. There were no apartment buildings or dwellings that would correspond to the urban settings in which the vast majority of the professional or formal jobs they sought were located. They wanted the best of both worlds—to live in a beautiful and safe part of the country, and yet with the jobs that are scarce or non-existent in their area.

Four decades ago, approximately two-thirds of the population lived in small towns and rural areas. With the decline of the agricultural economy, according to a study by PRISMA, the Salvadoran Research Program on Development and Environment, there are as many jobs in the metropolitan area of San Salvador as there are in the rest of the country. In addition, there are now more non-farming jobs in rural areas than farming jobs, and many of those are in areas such as commerce and services.

While one characteristic of the Salvadoran economy is the shift from rural to urban, another very significant attribute of the economy is the preponderance of informal workers/the informal economy. In the United States, informal workers are those who do not work for a particular employer or business and who do not report earnings for income tax purposes.* These workers are concentrated in agriculture, domestic service, or manual labor (and anyone who in their teen years has ever babysat or mowed lawns, got paid for this, and did not report the earnings was an informal worker). Individuals who contract with employers to perform work, such as freelance artists and consultants, and whose income is reported to government agencies but who do not receive any benefits from the employer, are considered to have nonstandard formal employment. In the United States, not counting undocumented workers, informal workers constitute far less than 5% of the total workforce.

In El Salvador, the informal economy is much more prominent. Many Salvadorans in the formal economy have access to a social security retirement systems and are a part of the ISSS health insurance system. However, not all workers in the formal economy are covered by these health and retirement benefits. The ISSS system was established in 1949, and a clarification in 1956 stipulated that agricultural workers were not covered. Because of this, and the large number of workers in the informal sector, only 28% of the more than 2.5 million Salvadorans in the work force are covered by these systems.

Just as the standards for formal work differ from country to country, so do the definitions of unemployment. According to 2012 census data, the unemployment rate in El Salvador was only 6.6 percent of the country. However, this includes both those who were employed full-time and those underemployed, and the full-time workers were only 57.3% of those counted as employed. Underemployed means those who were working part-time or sporadically and the largest group of the underemployed, 53.4%, who work in the informal sector. The informal sector includes all those who

*In the United States, it is important to make a distinction between undocumented workers, who do not work in the formal economy because of their immigration status, and other informal workers.

work in the large markets selling everything from food to electronics to clothes; in the large market in the center of San Salvador, this can be thousands of people. Douglas Jimenez, the tax auditor whose narrative is in the "Stories" section, told me that his parents supported themselves and their family selling underwear in a stand in the central market. The informal sector also includes the women and children who sell Chiclets or newspapers on street corners, taxi drivers, and anyone who does not receive a formal paycheck, in which case taxes would be taken out. The second largest group of the underemployed, 33.6%, works in the agricultural sector.

Working full-time in the formal sector does not guarantee a living wage. The minimum wage, last increased in 2013, is $224.29 monthly for retail employees, $219.40 for those who work in industrial factories, $187.68 for those who work in textile *maquilas*, and $104.97 for agricultural workers. The minimum wage has not kept up with inflation, and has only about a third as much buying power as it did in the mid-1970s.

Knowing how much one is paid is incomplete information unless one knows the cost of things. Comparing living costs between El Salvador and the United States, however, is difficult. It depends on where you are living and how you are eating. When I am in El Salvador, I spend more on gasoline than in the U.S. However, instead of going to a chain restaurant and spending $8 for a lunch, I can go to an informal diner, a *comedor*, and get a meal of meat, rice, and a vegetable for $2. I pay essentially the same at a supermarket in El Salvador as I do in the United States, but if I were to go to the market at the center of San Salvador, food is cheaper. And depending on the location of the dwelling, in small cities and some neighborhoods, one can rent a house for $60 a month.

So how does one understand how well individuals are doing economically in El Salvador? There is no one way. One approach is to compare average income with that of neighboring countries. Another is to examine how much of the total income of the country goes to individuals in the top fifth of earners, the second fifth, etc. This leads to a discussion of income inequality in the country, and what it means to be rich, middle class, and in poverty.

Comparing annual average income with its neighbors in the Northern Triangle of Central America, El Salvador's average of

$3590 per person is greater than Guatemala ($3120) and Honduras ($2120). However, in comparison with all Latin American and Caribbean developing countries, El Salvador falls far short of the $4,981 average annual income.

Figures on average annual income are only part of the picture. In El Salvador, the top 20% earn 53% of all income, with the next highest earning almost 21% of all income, meaning that they get all but about a quarter of all earnings in the country. The middle fifth earns almost 14% of all earnings, with the next-to-bottom fifth earning only 9% and the bottom fifth earning not even 4% of total earnings.

As those figures indicate, income inequality in El Salvador is high, and it is similar to other Latin American countries. The measure for assessing income inequality based on income distribution among individuals in a given economy is the Gini Index. A Gini Index of 0 represents perfect equality, while an Index of 100 implies perfect inequality. The countries on the low end of the Gini Index are Denmark, Sweden, Japan, and Norway, with a score around 25. Canada, with a Gini Index score of 32.5, ranks 46th. Income inequality has been lessening somewhat in El Salvador at the same time that income inequality in the United States has been growing, higher now than at any time since the 1920s. Consequently, the Gini scores are similar for El Salvador and the United States: 42.0 for the United States, 41.0 for El Salvador, both ranking among the most income-unequal countries.

A high degree of income inequality essentially means that there are some people with a lot of money and a lot of people with very little money. In El Salvador, there has been talk for decades of the Fourteen Families that supposedly control the country. Although this may be an arbitrary number—and like the list of the richest people in the country or the world, this can change somewhat over time—it is clear that there are some families with an extraordinary degree of economic power. These include families that have been in El Salvador for centuries, others that came to El Salvador early in the 20th century, and a third group of Christians from Palestine that came to El Salvador in the mid-20th century.

One of those families that would fit in the second group is the Poma family. Bartolomé Poma was a Spaniard who moved to El Salvador in 1918 and started a business selling Hudson and Essex automobiles. The business grew to include other automobile dealerships and real estate holdings. His son Ricardo, who has been CEO of this family-owned business for decades, earned his undergraduate and MBA degrees from Ivy League colleges before coming back to work in the family business. In an interview with the *New York Times* in 2010, talking about the years before the civil war, he said: "We were all thriving. I distinctly recall a day in 1977, having lunch at our family farm, sitting near a clear pond under a huge tree. Out of nowhere, Father said: 'We are so happy, so close, the business is doing well, El Salvador is progressing. When will the ax fall?'"

I read the interview, and the phrase "El Salvador is progressing" jumped out at me. The decades that he is referring to were ones of increased landlessness and income inequality. In 1961, only 19.8% of Salvadorans did not own any land; by 1971, that had increased to 41.1%. By 1980 the poorest fifth of the country earned just 2% of national income, a drop of almost half since 1970, and the richest fifth had 66% of national income. Ricardo Poma's statement that equates the country progressing with the prosperity of the family business reflects an insularity shared by many of the rich in El Salvador, an idea of the natural order in the world that is probably not shared with well over 95% of their countrymen. Governmental policies that favored the rich were instituted and maintained by the political party ARENA during the years when they controlled the presidency (1989–2009). There was no tax on dividends, and there still is no tax on the land one owns.

The government's annual Multiple Purpose Survey of Households reports the percentage of households at the other end of the economic spectrum. The 2012 publication puts the poverty rate for the country at 34.5%, with 8.9% in extreme poverty and 25.6% in relative poverty. Persons in rural areas were more likely to be poor than were urban residents. The poverty rates are determined based on the cost of buying a Basic Food Basket (*Canasta Básica Alimentaria* or CBA), which contains rice, beans, vegetables, fruit, meat, and tortillas. Extreme poverty is then defined as those households that earn less per month than the monthly cost of the CBA. Households considered to be in relative poverty earn less than twice the cost of the CBA. On the basis that food costs are lower in rural areas, in 2011, the CBA for urban households was set at $182.60 per month for an average household of 3.72 members, or $1.64 per person per day. For rural households, the CBA was set at $143.90 per month for an average household of 4.24 members, or $1.13 per person per day. The measure of poverty is inexact in that it is based on the cost of basic food items. When the cost of these go up, as happened in 2011 when the cost of beans skyrocketed, the CBA increases, and as a result, the number of people in poverty increases. When food costs go down, with a resulting decrease in the cost of the CBA, the number of people in poverty decreases (and governments can claim credit for reducing poverty).

Terms like "extreme poverty" and "relative poverty" are abstract. One indication of well being as contrasted with poverty is that only 67.2% of all households in rural areas have access to electric energy, and 66.4% have access to water systems that bring water to their house; the rest have to carry water from communal wells or streams.

There are the rich and the poor, but what about those in the middle? Defining middle class in any society is not easy. In El Salvador, the average monthly household income in 2012 was $506.91—$338.55 in rural households and $594.91 in urban households. Professional positions, ones that we think of as middle-class, often do not pay that well. A 2012 study on higher education found that faculty members, most with only an undergraduate degree, made between $500 and $1000 a month for full-time employment. Lucas, a social worker I know, is in his mid-40s, has an undergraduate degree in social work, and works for a government agency. He makes about $800 a month at that job, and sometimes gets part-time work to supplement his salary. He rents an apartment. While he owns a car, a 10-year-old Toyota, he takes the bus more than an hour each way to work because it is less expensive.

While it is difficult to determine the nature and extent of the middle class in El Salvador, one of the things that surprised me most when I came back to El Salvador in 2005, 33 years since my Peace Corps days there, were the changes in the capital city that appeared to be evidence of a growing middle class.

I observed the large numbers of fast food, mid-scale, and upscale restaurants; food chains; and three large malls—and at least two more have been constructed since then. When I lunch on a soup and sandwich at San Martín, a bakery and café in San Salvador, I see large numbers of Salvadorans dressed in the same kind of professional attire one would see in the U.S. In comparison with four decades ago, the streets of San Salvador are now crowded with cars as well as buses, and rush-hour traffic on a late Friday afternoon rivals most American cities.

It's not just that there are more people. One's perspective is shaped by one's own experience, and my take on the country as a Peace Corps Volunteer was that the country largely consisted of the poor, those just a half-step away from being poor, and the rich. One day in 1971, I was walking from the Peace Corps office in downtown San Salvador back to City Hall where I worked, taking a route different than the one I usually took. I glanced at a building and saw a sign for an architect—and stopped. I was not used to seeing indications of middle-class professionals. I also remember the time Don Miguel, the owner of the house in the poor neighborhood where I rented a room, borrowed a television. That night, watching a local television station, I saw an ad for Avis Car Rental. That ad, which in the United States I would probably not have noticed, seemed very foreign to my existence there, as I was living without running water or indoor plumbing, like a large proportion of Salvadorans at that time.

One of the reasons for the appearance of a sizable middle class comes from migration and its impacts. Although exact numbers on migration are hard to come by, it is widely accepted that around 30% of Salvadorans live in another country, and at least 20% of Salvadoran families receive remittances.

Remittances contribute to the reduction of poverty and a better life for those who receive them. As the 2007 census reported, 70% of those receiving remittances were not in poverty. Given that many of these are (or would be) the poorest families in the country, the impact on daily life of the remittances is substantial. One of the youths interviewed in my 2005 study *One Family, Two Countries* agonized over what it would be like if his mother would return: "It would be wonderful having her here, but we would not eat the same way we do now."

Of the families that receive remittances, almost all spend them on consumption (the purchase of goods and services): only 1.4% say they save some or all of the amount they receive.

Consumption of goods and services can mean that a family can send a child to school or have enough to eat. Receiving remittances can also mean that people have some disposable income, and can eat out and in other ways participate in a lifestyle that is somewhat middle class. Tim Muth, in his excellent *Tim's El Salvador Blog*, has an example of this:

> *El Salvador's commercial interests are structured to capture that remittance flow as much as they can. I learned about one example of this last week when I was in San Salvador. A friend pointed out the very large indoor playgrounds which accompany every fast food franchise in the city. Pizza Huts, Burger Kings, KFCs, Pollo Campero and more all have these big play areas, much larger than any you see in the US. My friend made the point that these fast food restaurants were always completely filled each weekend with birthday parties, and the birthday parties are all paid for directly by family members living abroad. The fast food operators make it easy for the families living abroad to order their birthday parties with online sites.*

In spending money from remittances or other sources on consumer goods, one sees a trend of consumerism not as present in earlier decades. The influence of Western (principally U.S.) preferences in food, in clothing, in music can now be seen not only in the capital city but throughout the country. We filmed interviews for the documentary I made in 2005, *Difficult Dreams,* in a very rural area of the department of Cabañas. In one remote community, I talked to one male in his late teens or early 20s who told me that he would cut sugar cane and harvest coffee beans at the times of the year when that work was available. His description of what he did was perhaps not dissimilar from that of his father and grandfather would have said if I had asked them decades ago, but the photo we took of him—in T-shirt, jeans, baseball cap—could just as well have been taken in East Oakland or Washington, D.C.

Anthropologist Suzanne Kent studied consumerism in El Salvador among middle-class families, which she categorizes as neither the very poor nor part of the wealthy elite. She refers to Falk and Campbell's concept of "the consumption of experience," in that the consumption of experience and the experience of consumption have become more and more indistinguishable. In her study, she examines the impact of the tension or contradiction between the promises of a consumption system—you will be happy if you purchase these shoes or this new phone—and the structural limitations of the Salvadoran economy that limit or exclude one from making the purchases. There exists a conflict between what they could imagine and what social life would permit.

Kent was told that people dress up in the best clothes that they have and go to Metrocentro, the biggest and most centrally located mall; there have been at least 10 additions since it first opened 4 decades ago. There is symbolic participation, according to Kent, by walking around a mall, window shopping and people watching, and perhaps eating a dish of ice cream before leaving. A step or two farther down on the economic ladder from the individual or family who can do this would be the teenager I saw one day walking through a food court at Metrocentro who picked up a half-eaten dish of ice cream and, still walking, finished it before he walked out of the food court.

Youth are aware of the constraints to employment. In Santacruz Giralt and Carranza's 2009 survey, 63% of youth said that there was little or no likelihood of their finding work. The slowdown in the Salvadoran economy seems to have had a greater impact on males than females. The percentage of male young adults working has dropped from 76% to 68% between 1990 and 2012. For women, there is greater participation than before in the work force, although a greater percentage of them are informal workers. Given that outlook, how do youth proceed? What happens to young people who cannot find jobs in El Salvador?

Some are called *ninis* (*ni estudia ni trabaja*)—neither studying nor working—and there are an estimated 241,000 of them between the ages of 15 and 25 in El Salvador. Alejandro, profiled in the "Stories" chapter, is among them. Chief reasons for their prevalence include the unavailability of safe and well-paying jobs; chief among concerns about them is their vulnerability to gang influence.

For youth, the route to employment would seem to lie in furthering one's education, as higher education is supposed to be a pathway to a better life. College enrollment increased 20% between 2006 and 2010 and 23.8% of those youth aged 24–29 interviewed in Ramos's nationwide study had attended or were attending post-secondary education. For many in El Salvador, though, getting an education does not lead to employment. Young adults who are unemployed have an average of 10 years of schooling, compared to 8.8 years of schooling for the employed. In some cases, youth do not continue their education if they see older siblings or cousins who have a high school or college degree and cannot find work.

I was curious about the degree of opportunity for those coming of age compared to the past, so I asked Mike Wise how this compared now from when he moved to El Salvador in 1981. Mike's an interesting guy. He flew helicopters for the U.S. Army in Viet Nam, and earned a doctorate in Agricultural Economics before starting to do international development work. He came down to El Salvador to work with the U.S. Embassy, married a Salvadoran, and stayed in the country working on various economic development projects. Mike has been involved in small business in El Salvador over the years and seems to know everybody. I met him in 2005, when he was the Peace Corps Director in El Salvador.

After thinking about the question for a couple of days, Mike said that it is almost a paradoxical situation. While there are far more opportunities, the chances of getting a good job if you are prepared are lower than they were decades ago. In his opinion, since there were only two universities in El Salvador in 1970 (the National University and the private University of Central America), the economy could absorb the relatively few graduates more easily. I checked out Mike's analysis of the situation by talking with one of the administrators at the small college in San Salvador with which I am affiliated, a civil engineer who graduated from the National University in the 1960s. His response to my question was: "Yes, when I graduated, I think that all the engineers in my class had jobs."

I have heard stories of qualified graduates not being able to find work from a variety of sources. When I met with teachers from

IEPROES, one of the leading technical institutes that prepare nurses, faculty members talked about the bad working conditions in some hospitals. Nurses may not complain, because they know, in the words of one of the teachers, "there are five other unemployed nurses waiting to take my spot." Andrés Dominguez, the Director of Health Promotion for three departments who occasionally interviews potential health promoters, laments the fact that, as he says, "I interview ten candidates; they could all do the work, and they all tell me how much they need the job."

If those in their 20s cannot find work, many of them still have expectations about the life they want to have. As a report from the United Nations Economic Commission for Latin America and the Caribbean stated, youth "have access to the images, icons, music, and modern messages, but they cannot translate this access into social mobility or into a complementary increase in wages and capacity to consume material goods and services."

The pull of *El Norte* can be strong when aspirations for a middle-class job and a middle-class lifestyle are frustrated after one has furthered one's education. Luís Romero, who worked with Homies Unidos, an organization that works with those who have left gangs, stated that while ex-gang members have trouble finding jobs, they are not the only ones: "They go to the university, they get their diplomas as professionals, but they cannot find a job. What do they do? Some just decide to migrate to California. They do not care that they have a degree, so they go to wash dishes or another kind of job in another country."

Will things get better for youth in El Salvador? Will there be more economic activities and more reason to stay in their own country? It is hard to say, as this small country is so affected by events in the larger world, such as the 2009 recession in the United States that caused a downturn in the Salvadoran economy. There are several factors, however, that could lead to greater economic activity and more opportunities for youth coming of age.

The United States and the European Union have been assisting El Salvador with improvements in the infrastructure of the country. Through a program known as the Millennium Challenge Corporation, the United States helped El Salvador build the Northern Transnational Highway in the western part of the country, running from the Pacific Ocean to Honduras, which is helping small businesses get their products to market. There may be additional support through the Millennium Challenge in the future to develop coastal and maritime areas. El Salvador is also one of the four countries that is participating with the United States in the Partnership for Growth program, which seeks to help countries increase their exports while maintaining a commitment to sustainable development and human rights. As the U.S. Embassy in El Salvador reports, this compact "represents the largest concerted economic development program in the Western Hemisphere. In its first four years of implementation, $379.5 million have already been invested in four broad project areas: education and training, community development, productive development, and road connectivity."

Investment from Salvadorans living in the United States may be a key to promoting economic growth in El Salvador. A large number of Salvadorans, especially those who migrated during the years of the civil war who now are citizens or legal residents, own small and medium-size businesses. One of the initiatives of the Funes administration, supported by the Millennium Challenge Corporation, was to encourage these Salvadorans living abroad to invest not only their dollars but their business expertise in their home country.

If immigration reform in the United States leads to a larger number of Salvadorans who are now undocumented achieving legal status, which would allow them to travel freely between the United States and El Salvador, it is likely that a number of them would become economically involved in El Salvador. In a study of Salvadorans under 30—all undocumented—living in the Washington, D.C. area, anthropologist Joseph Wiltberger asked "what their plans and desires would be if they were legally permitted to travel between El Salvador and the United States at will." In their responses, says Wiltberger,

Their ideas and imaginations were strikingly consistent: most

explicitly expressed an interest in generating employment opportunities for others in their community of origin through creative businesses that would draw on resources acquired while living in the US. Ideas varied from starting restaurants to creating businesses providing not-yet-available services to pioneering new farming operations.

It is difficult to predict how much investment and assistance will come from Salvadorans living abroad in the near future, and also how much difference the recent investment in highway construction will make in the possibilities of jobs for youth unsure of their futures. For the United States and other donor nations, it could make sense to focus some efforts specifically on how development funds could benefit the job prospects of youth coming of age.

9

Violence

I was in El Salvador for 10 days in May 2013 finishing up interviews for this book. I spent a day and a half on the coast before returning home. In the van going to the airport that Sunday morning, as I was talking with the driver, we saw police cars on the other side of the road and slowed down. The reason for their presence was a dead young woman, largely unclothed, who had been dumped by the side of the road. That image does not leave me.

When I tell people that I spend three weeks or so a year in El Salvador studying the issues of youth, those people who do know about El Salvador largely associate the country with the violence of the civil war several decades ago or connect it with gangs that are spilling over to the U.S. The first question they then often ask, with concern in their voice, is: "How safe is it there?"

It's a good question, and I usually answer it by replying, "Do you mean how safe is it for me when I am in El Salvador, or how safe is it for people in general there?" These are two separate questions, and in this chapter, I will answer both of them. I will give a somewhat detailed account of the origin of the gangs that are responsible for much of the concern about safety and also discuss the growing problem of organized crime. Then, as in other chapters in this section, I will describe how gangs and violence affect youth, and bring in the perspectives of the youth profiled in the "Stories" chapter.

What strikes you when you first come to San Salvador are the razor wire and the number of security guards. There is razor wire on the tops of the walls and on roofs. There are *vigilantes*, security guards, outside most commercial establishments and hotels and on many residential streets. Our son's reaction to this while living there in 2005 was, "An armed guard outside Burger King?" These *vigilantes* generally carry shotguns or automatic weapons. For the most part, they are paid minimum wage, less than $200 a month, and I am not sure how strong a deterrent they actually are. In the mornings when I am in San Salvador, I walk in the Parque Maquilishuat, a thin park with gorgeous flowers and stately trees that has a third-mile paved trail used by both runners and walkers. There are cars parked up and down the street by 7:30 a.m. In April, 2012, a car full of heavily armed men drove up and started breaking into cars. One warned the *vigilante* who appeared: "Stay away, old man." The security guard stood down and did not do anything until the thieves left.

How safe do I feel in El Salvador? I wrote this on one of my twice-yearly visits:

> It is Sunday morning, half an hour past daybreak. I am walking through the neighborhood where I stay in San Salvador when I am here to get to the Parque Maquilishuat. There is a major commercial thoroughfare a couple of blocks away, with shops and chain restaurants. On these streets, in a country where zoning rules are non-existent, middle-class homes alternate with shops, doctor's offices, and small restaurants.
>
> It is peaceful, and as I go out for a run or brisk walk, I feel no different than I would if I were downtown in any major American city in the morning. I watch out for traffic, but my eyes and my adrenal system are not straining for potential danger.
>
> Even in this relatively safe area, it feels different at night. Night always comes shortly after 6 p.m. In 2005, when we lived in El Salvador, in the same neighborhood, when I would go out to a restaurant or to buy a bottle of wine after dark, I would be on high alert, hyper-aware of what was around me. Shortly

*after we got back to the states in December of that year, after
6 months in El Salvador, I walked out one night to go to the
public library, a few blocks from our house. Almost immediately, I felt my heart begin to beat much faster. I started to
laugh at myself. We live in a neighborhood where people don't
always lock their doors when they leave, but my body was still
in the El Salvador mode of high alert when walking at night.*

On the whole, El Salvador is a dangerous place. In 2011, it was
ranked 2nd for most homicides per capita in the world. It was still
ranked high in 2012, when the number of murders dropped sharply.

There are places in the country where violence and the threat
of violence are a way of life. But some areas being unsafe does not
mean that all areas are unsafe. In many areas of the capital city, in
parts of the countryside, in many small towns, violence and murder are rare events. My friend Mike Wise has lived in El Salvador
for more than three decades, working with USAID and then as the
Peace Corps Director before retiring in the country. He says that
neither he nor any of his family has ever been directly affected by
violence. That has been the experience of other Salvadoran friends,
and also mine in the times that I have been there.

Travel websites like the Lonely Planet state that attacks on tourists are rare, and that they consider El Salvador as safe as the rest of
Central America. England's *Telegraph* named El Salvador one of the
top 20 travel destinations for 2014 and did not mention threats to
personal security. At the start of this chapter, I mentioned seeing a
body on the side of the road; I had been coming from a beachfront
area with Tourist Police patrol, where young surfers party late with
little concern for their safety.

While the country is relatively safe for the somewhat privileged
and for tourists, how safe is it for many Salvadorans? I think of the
adage: "Where you stand (on an issue) depends on where you sit."
In El Salvador, it's where you happen to be that often determines
how safe you feel.

This was brought home to me on a late June afternoon in 2011.
Julio, a taxi driver I employed when in the country, took me to San
Marcos, a small city 35 minutes from San Salvador. As a part of a
study we were conducting on youth and migration there, I was go-

ing to do a background information interview with a young doctor who does volunteer work with youth in the community.

The doctor was late, and Julio and I stood on a corner waiting, in a neighborhood neither rich nor poor. Julio was alert: "I don't like it here."

"But look," I said, "there are children running around, people stopping and talking, noise."

Julio responded: "It could all change in a moment, and when it does, everyone will be inside, the doors closed, and afterwards, no one saw anything."

Indeed, in talking with the doctor when he showed up, it turned out that three people were shot on that corner a few months earlier. No one was charged with or convicted for the killing, as in approximately 95% of the murders in El Salvador.

If you compare personal safety between El Salvador and the United States by looking at the numbers, El Salvador is far more violent—38.4 murders occur per 100,000 people in El Salvador (2012), as compared to the 4.7 murders per 100,000 people in the U.S. in the same year. Yet where one lives in both countries must be taken into account, and one's sense of personal safety depends not on national murder rates but on one's exact location. There are areas of El Salvador that are safe, while the murder rates in some cities in the U.S. are far too high—such as the 53 deaths per 100,000 citizens in Detroit and 54.2 per 100,000 in New Orleans in 2012.

Until recently, most of the violence in El Salvador was concentrated in urban areas such as San Marcos, but violence and insecurity have spread into the outlying urban communities that have grown fast in recent decades—places where you can buy a small house for $20,000 or less (house and condo prices in upscale areas of San Salvador are comparable to major U.S. cities). Roxana, a teacher in her late 20s at the Universidad Panamericana, told me about an incident in her community. Her family lives in Soyapango, one of those communities where one can buy a small house for $15,000. One afternoon she was walking back to her house with her sister and niece. Moments after they entered, there were gunshots just outside. The woman who sold bread on the corner and people buying from her were shot multiple times and killed, because the woman had not paid off the local gang. Roxana was trembling as she recounted this: "We got down on the floor with my niece, telling her it was fireworks. If we had been a minute later getting to the house . . . ."

The violence has infiltrated more remote areas as well. In 2007, there were roughly two urban murders for every one murder in the rural areas of El Salvador. But by 2013, the number of murders committed in rural areas exceeded those in the urban centers. This shift matches what I have heard anecdotally, that the gangs have been gradually moving out of urban neighborhoods and into rural communities, pushed there by police sweeps and military patrols.

I was conducting a workshop in El Salvador for college/university researchers in 2011, and during a break one of the participants said to me, "You know, it's worse now than during the war." I have heard that other times. Ellen Moodie, in her book *El Salvador in the Aftermath of Peace*, writes that from the mid-1990s on, individual Salvadorans would make that comparison: "it's worse than the war." While the number of homicides associated with gangs in the past decade in El Salvador does not come close to the 70,000 killed in the civil war, I can understand the comparison.

For one thing, there were parts of the country where the fighting between the Armed Forces and the guerrillas did not reach. In the areas in which there was fighting, it was not continuous. The capital, San Salvador, only experienced fighting toward the end of the war. A friend who was a college student in San Salvador during the war once told me that during the guerrilla offensive they would listen to the radio in the morning to learn where there had been bombings in order to learn if they needed to take an alternate route to the university. Her account was strikingly similar to someone talking about listening to a traffic report in order to redirect one's route to avoid congestion.

When Salvadorans now talk about feeling safe or unsafe, the conversation usually refers to gangs. The presence and actions of gang members have both affected and preoccupied Salvadorans for over a decade. The Salvadoran Security Ministry in May 2013 identified 1,955 *clicas*—small gang units identified with the major gangs, and suggested that each *clica* has a minimum of 15 members, which would mean that there are at least 29,325 gang members on the street.

How the gangs became such a powerful force in Salvadoran

society is a story of at least two cases of the "unanticipated effects of actions," a concept that sociologist Robert Merton popularized in the first decades of the 20th century. Actions can sometimes have unanticipated negative effects that can at times outweigh the positive ones. One example of this was the way that U.S. immigration laws helped create Salvadoran gangs. A second was a policy decision years later by the El Salvador government to separate the gangs in prison, which led to the gangs gaining power and influence.

The best description I have heard of the origin of gangs in El Salvador came from a Salvadoran, now a U.S. citizen, who has lived in Los Angeles for more than 25 years. We met at a hotel in the beautiful small town of Suchitoto when he was visiting his homeland, and he described it this way:

> When the war came, both the Army and the guerrillas were forcibly recruiting boys 16 and older, sometimes younger. So families would send the young men to the United States, sometimes before they started fighting, sometimes afterwards. So they go across the border mojado (undocumented) and go to Los Angeles. They were living in the poor areas of LA, like South Central, and they were getting harassed by the African-American gangs there, the Bloods and Crips. The recently arrived Salvadorans look around and see that the black gang members have knives and little puny guns—pistols. Some of these Salvadoran kids, they've fought in the civil war, they're used to AK-47s, so they get themselves some bigger guns.

These newly arrived adolescents formed the Mara Salvatrucha (As Ana Arana explains in an article called "How the Street Gangs Took Central America," "*Mara*" is Salvadoran slang for gangs, "*Salva*" for El Salvador, and "*trucha*"—literally "trout" in English—is slang for "clever" or "a shrewd person"). The gang is generally referred to as MS-13. Other young Salvadorans in Los Angeles were recruited into a Mexican-American gang, Barrio 18 (or M-18 or 18th Street gang), named after the 18th Street area.

A number of these gang members, as they got more involved in illegal activities, were arrested. In the 1990s, penalties for criminal behavior in the U.S. were getting tougher (as in the "three strikes you're out" rule). In 1996, Ana Arana explains,

Congress extended the get-tough approach to immigration law. Noncitizens sentenced to a year or more in prison would now be repatriated to their countries of origin, and even foreign-born American felons could be stripped of their citizenship and expelled once they served their prison terms. The list of deportable crimes was increased, coming to include minor offenses such as drunk driving and petty theft.

Among the Salvadoran gang members who were deported were many who had come to the U.S. as young children of families fleeing the war and were native English speakers.

When the deportees arrived in El Salvador, many had few skills, and some spoke little Spanish. What the MS-13 and M-18 gang members had was their gang connections. According to Arana:

Local governments—which were desperately trying to rebuild after a decade of civil strife—had no idea who their new citizens really were: the new U.S. immigration rules banned U.S. officials from disclosing the criminal backgrounds of the deportees.

The result, predictably, was a disaster. At first, few Central American officials paid attention to the new arrivals. But the returnees, with their outlandish gang tattoos, their Spanglish, and their antiauthoritarian attitudes, soon made themselves noticed. Shortly after their arrival, crack cocaine was introduced to El Salvador, and related arrests, which had been in the single digits in 1995, climbed to 286 three years later. ... "We had these guys arriving in fresh territory and they did what they knew how to do best," said Lou Covarrubiaz, a former San José police chief turned police trainer in El Salvador.

Starting in the early 2000s, successive Salvadoran presidents put into place repressive policies to combat the gangs, with few positive results. In July, 2003, then-President Francisco Flores announced a police-military "get-tough" policy, named Mano Dura or "Iron Fist." This Anti-Gangs Act was passed by the legislature, but parts of it were determined to be unconstitutional by the Supreme Court the following year, including a provision that authorized detention and punishment based on membership in a group or on the way you looked.

Flores' successor, Tony Saca, introduced his anti-gang initiative, *Super Mano Dura* or "Super Iron Fist." This continued the policy of locking up suspected gang members, but also allocated funds and sought support from international donors for violence prevention efforts and reinsertion into society of rehabilitated gang members. However, 80% of funds went toward law enforcement.

In 2009, Mauricio Funes became the first president from the FMLN, the guerrilla group that became a political party after the end of the civil war. He continued the policies of his predecessors, and deployed military units to share policing duties in high crime areas. During his term, the army grew by more than 50%, to 17,000 soldiers in mid-2012.

What has been the impact of these get-tough policies? They did not decrease the violence in the country. The homicide rate went from 43.4 per 100,000 residents in 2004 to 55.5 in 2005, to 92.3 in 2008, and then to 71 in 2011. Then, in early 2012, talks mediated by a conservative bishop, a former general now in charge of the National Police force, and an ex-guerrilla commander led to a gang truce. In 2012, the homicide rate went from 14 to 5 or 6 a day, and in 2013, there were 104 fewer homicides than the year before—the least violent year since 2003. Relations in the prisons also improved in 2012 and 2013, with violence rates in the prisons dropping. The gang leaders were transferred to a prison with slightly better conditions (El Salvador's prisons have been compared to those in Haiti and the Congo) but there do not appear to have been other overt concessions for those in prison.

The impacts of the ineffective Iron Fist policies perhaps could have been anticipated. Most experts credit the increased sophistication and greater reach of the two major gangs in large part to the law enforcement crackdowns and prison policies. According to analysis by InSight Crime, while prisoners are segregated by gang in order to reduce the number of violent incidents, this just "intensified the process of regrouping, as the gangs were safer and had more time to focus on expanding their activities, building nationwide extortion networks." In 2012, one municipality even told prisoners' families to bring them "uniforms"—white or yellow clothing, depending on which gang they were affiliated with. Thus segregating prisoners by gang affiliation has also had the unintended consequence of increasing recruitment in prison—inmates not previously in gangs have to decide which one to join.

Certainly, actions by both the United States and El Salvador over a span of two decades have contributed to the growth of gangs. However, gangs would not have been able to recruit to grow to the size they are now if it were not for domestic and economic conditions in the country. Governments in the 1990s, after the end of the civil war, did not invest in social services, education, or job training. For many youth in poor neighborhoods, a combination of coercion to join gangs and the perceived lack of other opportunities both contribute to decisions to become part of a gang.

Alma Guillermoprieto, a Mexican journalist, has documented this view of the narrowing of options for Latin American youth in poor neighborhoods. In a 2011 article in the *New York Review of Books,* she recounts the perspective of Howard Cotto, sub-director of investigations for the National Civil Police:

> A [gang member's] life is very short. They get sentenced to thirty years in no time. But in this country, as they see it, they have two choices: you can be a loser and keep on studying, and let's see if you can find a job once you've graduated, or you can be a powerful man by the time you're fourteen or seventeen. You can give orders, be in charge of distributing drugs in the neighborhood. You won't have to give your elders any respect, you'll be the one who can say to a neighbor, "You're going to leave this barrio this minute," and then take over his house. You'll be able to say to that girl you like and who doesn't like you, "You know what, whether you like it or not you're going to be mine, or whoever else's I decide."

The insecurity in El Salvador for many comes not just from the fear of being attacked physically or being robbed but also from the prevalence of extortion. According to experts, extortion—demanding money in return for a business, individual, or family member not being harmed—is the chief source of income for gang members, although the practice of extortion probably goes beyond gangs.

The practice of extortion is most visible with bus drivers, especially those whose routes take them through low-income neighborhoods or rural areas. A gang member will get on the bus and demand the weekly *renta* (payoff). If it is not paid, the driver can be shot—and several times the buses have been burned with passengers on board if the *renta* was not paid. Bus service in El Salvador is completely private, and there are more than 15,000 bus drivers who work with a number of companies, while others are self-employed. In 2009 (the latest figures), the bus drivers and owners paid more than 36 million dollars in "protection payments"—more than before the gang truce went into effect.

Extortion affects bus transportation in more than just urban areas. A Peace Corps Volunteer in a small town in the eastern part of the country told me of someone in his community who had risen from being a bus driver to owning two buses. He was approached the year before about paying *la renta*, and when he refused, he was shot. A few weeks later, the buses were back in operation, with the son in charge, and the assumption was that payments were being made.

An example of extortion comes from Mejicanos, a metropolitan area just outside the capital of San Salvador. Journalist Alma Guillermoprieto describes a conversation:

> I was chatting one afternoon with a particularly lively woman—let's call her María—who started to tell me how CINDE [a day care and after-school program] and the microloan program it manages had changed her life, because she now had a cart in which to trundle her wares back and forth, when two boys who looked to be around fifteen years old arrived at her stand. She cut the conversation short as the kids selected some of her wares and left without any money changing hands. Maria's eyes flickered with terror when I asked her if she was being renteada, or extorted, by the mareros. "Not really, not really," she whispered, looking at me pleadingly. "They don't ask me for money. Not yet. Just...little gifts."

I was talking with Mauricio Aracón, a Salvadoran who had left during the war, who is now a U.S. citizen and school teacher in northern Virginia. He comes back to El Salvador once or twice a year. He told me about visiting a friend in a small town on the ocean. After a good lunch, looking out to sea, he told his friend: "This is peaceful. I could retire here." His friend replied, shaking his head, "*Todo está renteado*" (everyone is paying extortion).

Extortion goes beyond being approached in communities. People receive phone calls demanding money or they will be killed. It's hard to know if it is from a gang or just from someone wanting to take advantage of fear. A friend of mine with a small consulting firm in San Salvador does not list her phone number or address in the website. She can be contacted through the website, and the website does not reveal information to potential extortionists. I was told of one strategy to avoid extortion calls, of a person whose landline answering machine message is "National Police Headquarters. Please leave a message." His friends understand the game that is being played and leave messages while potential extortionists are deterred.

I was in the city of Ilobasco, conducting interviews and taking photos, and wanted to take photos of people in line to get money from an ATM, the way that people receive remittances from the states from family members. My friend Andrés who lives there said no, that people would think that we were criminals taking photos to find out who has money and then to extort them. The photographer had a very good telephoto lens, so we were able to get the photos without alarming anyone, and the interchange was a good reminder of the extent of extortion.

I realized the impact of extortion in poor communities when talking with an ambitious young woman, who had become the assistant manager of a small beachfront hotel in her early 20s. She told me about having bought a small house for her mother, and another one, which she is renting out now. When I asked if she had a car, her reply was, "I know people in my community who had a small store. They came for extortion, ending up killing at least one person. If you have a car, people think that you have money. I won't buy a car now."

When I am in El Salvador, conversations about crime focus largely on gangs. However, experts on crime and violence at the Washington Office on Latin America are at least as concerned about the potential impact of drug trafficking and organized crime on El Salvador. In September 2011, the U.S. government added El Salvador and Belize to its list of major drug producing or drug-transit countries. According to BBC news, the inclusion of Belize and El Salvador on the list "reflects the growing influence of Mexico's powerful drugs cartels" and "in El Salvador in particular, the Mexican cartels are thought to be forming alliances with street gangs." An indication that gangs are getting more involved in drug trafficking is that the amount of cocaine seized in El Salvador doubled from 2012 to 2013. But another major player is the Texis Cartel—not a violent gang but the creation of legitimate businessmen and elected officials. The group controls a vital cocaine transit route through the country. The National Police Force (PCN) is also under scrutiny with charges of police corruption. The PCN was constituted after the civil war to replace the previous police force, which was complicit in torture and assassinations during that struggle. According to Hector Silva of the Center for Latin American and Latino Studies at American University, high-ranking police officers routinely protect those involved with drug shipments of cocaine across El Salvador.

This chapter has focused so far on Salvadorans in general. How does crime and violence affect Salvadoran youth and those in their 20s? This chapter differs from others in this section in that there are few clear positives. Youth are those most affected by violence—the majority of those killed are between 18 and 30—and they are concerned. In Ramos's nationwide survey, where youth were asked to list their principal concern, the top one was gangs (22.9%), the second was crime (21.3%), and the fourth was violence (12.7%)—almost 57% of the respondents listed these as the top problems. The lack of employment was the only other issue that got more than 15%.

A positive aspect is the absence of violence in remote rural areas, such as Hacienda Vieja, in the state of Chalatenango, near the Honduran border. In the studies that we have conducted there, almost universally both youth and adults have stated that one of the advantages of living there is the sense of personal security—one can walk around the community at any time without worry.

However, this area and other isolated similar communities are also ones which lack good roads and have few educational opportunities or jobs. The perception that this area is much safer than the rest of the country also serves as a detriment to leaving. One of the young women we interviewed was offered a college scholarship to attend a small private university in San Salvador. There was a relative living in San Salvador with whom this young woman could live, so attending college was affordable. However, this high school graduate's mother began having nightmares about her daughter being attacked in San Salvador, and finally the family decided that she would not be going off to attend college.

Violence spills over from the communities into the schools, affecting students and teachers. In 2011, 139 school students and 6 teachers were murdered. Within the schools, some gang members have been extorting other children. And a friend of mine who works closely with school teachers and principals around the country recalls that during a meeting, one of the principals told a story of teachers being confronted by gang members with the threat: "If you don't pass me even though I will do no work, we will kill you."

Living in a community known for gang violence also affects one's ability to find a job. Employers are often unwilling to hire youth from such neighborhoods, even when they come with strong references, for fear of gangs infiltrating or getting knowledge about their business.

In conducting research and talking with young Salvadorans, I learned of other effects of the violence and lack of personal security that I had not anticipated. In a focus group with high school students in San Vicente, I asked how violence had affected them. One student stated—and almost all the rest immediately seconded—that the preoccupation with safety has affected the relationships with their parents. The students considered themselves "street smart," knowing how to avoid dangerous areas, while their parents had more restrictive ideas about when it is safe for the high school students to be out.

Even for those who feel safe in their own low-income communities, the extortion of bus drivers and the possibility of violence on buses affect the majority of Salvadorans who use public transportation to get from place to another. Antonio, the bartender who is profiled in the "Stories" section, tells me that there is no insecurity in his neighborhood and he feels safe when he gets to work; it's on the 10-mile ride from one place to the other where he worries. Peace Corps Volunteers (PCVs) in El Salvador in 2012 were forbidden to use buses because of security concerns, and a van service now picks up PCVs when they need to come to the capital city.

Salvadorans who do not live in troubled neighborhoods and who have cars do not face the same degree of danger, but still have to be mindful of risks. Elisa, whose account is in the "Stories" chapter, replied to my question about safety by saying: "I don't wear expensive jewelry; I know which areas I can walk around at night by myself and which areas I need to be more careful, etc. Same things I would do in New York City, Cape Town, Oakland, etc."

When I think about the impact of living in situations where violence is common, I worry about the cumulative effect of this stress on young people. For those youth who live in neighborhoods or communities with gang involvement, there is not only the personal risk but also many occasions in which they are close to violent acts or have seen the results of such violence. In Santacruz Giralt and Carranza's 2009 National Survey of Youth (ages 15–24), those surveyed were asked if they had been victims at least once during the past 12 months of any of a number of different attacks. For males, 11.6% had been robbed by someone who was armed, and 5.4% had been threatened with being killed. One effect of this can be the normalization of violence—accepting it as just a part of life. When I asked the young woman that I referred to earlier who did not want to buy a car for fear of extortion about violence in her community, she replied matter-of-factly: "Not bad; from time to time they kill someone."

I am also concerned about the long-term impact of stress and of being on high alert. According to the American Psychological Association:

> An extreme amount of stress can take a severe emotional toll. While people can overcome minor episodes of stress by tapping into their body's natural defenses to adapt to changing situations, excessive chronic stress, which is constant and

persists over an extended period of time, can be psychologically and physically debilitating.

Unlike everyday stressors, which can be managed with healthy stress management behaviors, untreated chronic stress can result in serious health conditions including anxiety, insomnia, muscle pain, high blood pressure and a weakened immune system.

I want to go back to a statement I made early in the chapter: that in El Salvador, it's where you happen to be that often determines how safe you feel. In some ways, it's more complicated than that. The possibility of violence in low-income urban communities is clearly a concern for residents—the accounts of Rebeca and Maria Rosa in the "Stories" section illustrate this. However, there are low-income communities and neighborhoods which have bad reputations where the residents report being safe—there are young men who are gang members who live in those communities, but who do not bring their gang involvement into the neighborhoods where they live. Also from the "Stories" chapter, Douglas, who now has the kind of job as an auditor with the Finance Ministry where he and his family could live elsewhere if he chooses, tells me that he stays in the community because it is his home, and he knows the gang members and they know him. "We play *futbol* (soccer) together," he says. As Luís, too, recounts, he feels comfortable living in his neighborhood: "They are neighbors as well as gang members."

It's complicated—not all areas that seem safe are without violence, and not all distressed communities are dangerous for those who live there. But there are far too many tragedies, far too many situations that end like that of the young woman whose body I saw dumped by the side of the road, or of Danny, who, as Daniel recounts in the "Stories" chapter, had difficulty being accepted after serving time in prison and ended up being killed, perhaps because he had gone from one neighborhood in Barrio 18 territory to take out a girl who lived in another neighborhood in MS-13 territory. Perhaps the girl was a gang member's girlfriend. In any case, his death was unjustified.

CONCLUSION

10

Looking toward the Future

As the previous chapters have indicated, the challenges that Salvadorans face as they come of age in these liquid times are daunting. In this chapter, after placing the difficulties that they encounter in the context of young people in other parts of the world, I want to focus on the strengths and resources of young Salvadorans. Following that, I will discuss things that individual Salvadorans, their government, and other governments could do to support youth and young adults in moving forward. To conclude the chapter and book, I will also discuss how the actions and choices that these youth and young adults make will impact their lives and their country.

While the road to a good adulthood for Salvadoran youth is not an easy one, to varying degrees their difficulties are shared by young people in other parts of the world. In Europe in 2013, the unemployment rate rose to 24.4% for those under 25, with 41% unemployment for those under 25 in Italy, and 57% in Spain. In China, says journalist Keith Bradsher, young college graduates are four times as likely to be unemployed as people who only completed elementary school. There is a "structural mismatch" between the jobs that are available in manufacturing and the more white-collar aspirations of millions of recent college graduates, according to Ye Zhihong, a deputy secretary general of China's Education Ministry.

In the United States, economist Robert Samuelson posed the question in 2012: "Is the economy creating a lost generation?" Of those unemployed, underemployed, and looking for work, he says, 41% were 30 or younger, although they only comprise 27% of the labor force. College graduates who have been underemployed or unemployed for 2 years or more worry about their ability to compete with recent grads—and the more experienced unemployed—for jobs in their fields.

Yes, young Salvadorans are not alone in facing difficulties, and in each country the challenges are different. For Salvadorans coming of age, many of them have resources and strengths that assist them in the transition to a pleasing adulthood.

For those Salvadorans who receive remittances, this is clearly a resource. The chapter "Education" detailed the impact on youth who receive remittances on being in school. In the "Stories" section, the two individuals who are professionals were both supported by mothers who had emigrated to the United States, achieved legal status, and supported their children's education. In the case of Luís, his mother supported his college education in El Salvador. In Elisa's situation, she was able to legally go to the United States after high school graduation, where she earned a college degree before returning to El Salvador.

Having family members working abroad can assist in ways other than the support for education. In the "Family" chapter, I present findings from my study on youth who had at least one parent living in the United States, *One Family, Two Countries*. In that study, we used a schema of categories of youth whose parents were abroad developed by researchers Elana Zilberg and Mario Lungo to describe the 33 youth in our study. These categories were:

- Abandoned: youth who hope to be reunited with family with little evidence that this will happen;

- Hopeful: youth who have parent(s) in the U.S. making plans for reunification;

- Frustrated Hopeful: youth who have tried unsuccessfully to make it to the U.S. or are waiting for money to pay a smuggler to get them across the border; and

- Rooted: youth with parent(s) in the United States who have no intention of emigrating, and who have used the remittances for educational opportunities.

Among the 17 youth we interviewed who fell into the category "Rooted" were 3 males who could be put into a sub-group that we called "Very Rooted." All of these were living with their grandparents, studying in high school, and planning to go to college. The three grandfathers had small businesses—raising cattle, buying and selling cars, and operating a small store. The capital for these businesses comes from relatives in the United States, especially the parents of the youth. These three youth all report working with their grandparents in the business as well as going to school. When asked about their future plans, the three stated that they not only planned to finish college and start their professional careers but also to start small businesses. The hands-on experience they had had in a business and the potential for business capital from parents working abroad give youth in this situation another option for getting ahead or getting by in El Salvador if the college degree does not lead to employment. Other youth in the country with similar experiences also have that advantage.

Another support and resource, as shown by comprehensive national surveys of adolescents and young adults, is religion. The 2009 study by Santacruz Giralt and Carranza showed that more than three quarters of Salvadoran adolescents and young adults consider religion to be a "very important" aspect of their lives. In Ramos's 2011 national study of those aged 15–29, 54% of females and 46% of males said they attended church at least once a week, and another 12% of both genders attended at least once a month. In that study, 30.5% of Salvadoran youth reported participating in religious groups. The next highest participation rate was for athletic teams, with 23.5%; no other group had more than a 10% participation rate.

One inevitable result of any research project is that those carrying out the research wish, after the fact, that they had asked additional questions or sought out other information. The main regret that I have in the studies that I and my colleague Virginia Quintana carried out is that we did not seek to understand the role of religion and spirituality in the lives of youth and young adults. Alejandro, in the chapter "Stories," brought this up, but we did not ask about it with others.

It is not only religious practices but also spirituality that can be a resource for youth—even those who are considered by much of Salvadoran society as beyond the reach of religion and faith. In a study of youth who were gang members and youth at great risk for gang involvement, it was found that among youth for whom spirituality and to a lesser degree religious coping were present, there was less alcohol and illegal drug use.

In the excellent recent book *Homies and Hermanos: God and Gangs in Central America*, Ron Brenneman writes about his interviews with 63 former gang members, many of whom who had successfully exited the "marriage to death" of gang membership through their involvement with small evangelical churches. Dr. Brenneman tells stories of former gang members whose conversion to Christianity, as practiced by small evangelical churches in rough neighborhoods, had given them another identity and community; in some instances it also made their exit from the gang more acceptable to gang members. In belonging to a church where complete abstinence from drugs and alcohol and strict morals are required, others in the community could easily tell if the ex-gang member was serious about being an *evangelico* or just playing the part to leave the gang.

Another resource is the optimism of youth. It may be the nature of the young to be optimistic about the future. I remembered reading a few years ago Jonathon Kozol's book *Ordinary Resurrections: Children in the Years of Hope*, about children in a low-income community in the South Bronx. According to Kozol:

> *They live, admittedly, in what is known as a "bad section" of a racially divided city, but they live as well within the miniature and often healing world that children of their age inhabit everywhere in the United States. Statistical curses—dangerous words like "AIDS," "incarceration," "needle drugs," "deficient school performance"—stand around them like unfriendly social scientists with cold prophetic powers; but the actual kingdom that they live in for a good part of each day is not the*

*land of bad statistics but the land of licorice sticks and long
division, candy bars and pencil sets, and Elmo dolls…*

The adolescents and emerging adults in this book are older
than those Kozol wrote about, and yet there is optimism about the
future. I found this in focus groups with both adolescents and
young adults in rural areas and in the cities of San Vicente and
Santa Ana. In Ramos's 2011 nationwide survey of Salvadoran
youth, 79.2% said they felt the future would be "better than the
present," with fewer than 10% stating that in the future they would
be looking for work, and fewer than 10% stating that they would
be living in another country. Those in urban areas were more optimistic than those in rural areas, and those who were older were
less optimistic than younger ones.

The strong connections with family, as discussed in the "Family" chapter, can be seen as a strength and resource for youth. This
comes from frequent contact and support from family members,
whether in El Salvador or living abroad. And the characteristics
that led to El Salvador's ranking third in the world in happiness/
perception of well being appear to be present in younger as well as
older Salvadorans.

There are resources and strengths apparent in the accounts in
the "Stories" section. I am aware that in this small, unrepresentative
sample, the percentage of young adults who are "making it" is far
higher than it is in the general population. One of the drawbacks
of having a high ratio of stories in which the individuals are doing
well is that the reader could think: "If this person can make it, there
must be something wrong with others who are not similarly suc-
ceeding." There is a tendency to look at how well a person is doing
only through the lens of his or her own abilities and motivation. In
the language of social psychology, this is called the Fundamental
Attribution Error: over-associating someone's behavior with internal characteristics while paying insufficient attention to external
factors. While a number of those young adults profiled are very talented individuals, the role of supportive individuals and programs
in their success should be apparent in these narratives.

Connected to the resources and strengths of youth is a different
kind of a positive that can be a deciding factor in whether young

Salvadorans stay or leave: *arraigo*, or connectedness. In the "Migration" chapter, the push and pull factors of migration were introduced—what impels people to leave a country, what attracts them about another country. One can also think of stay factors—the aspects of living in a particular place that make one not want to leave.

Family certainly is one of these things, although less so if much of your family already lives in the States. For many people, it is involvement with a church, a civic organization, a theater group, or an athletic team. In this context, I want to mention Alejandro and Thelma from the "Stories" chapter. Alejandro could be categorized as a *nini*, one of those young adults who neither works nor is in school. A graduate from a 2-year technical school, he has big dreams of founding an Internet company. However, he also is very involved in his local church, and it is the connection with church and family that lead him to not be interested in migrating. Thelma has managed to find college scholarships through her involvement with community groups, and her interest is in serving the local communities in her area. There is not stable funding to do this—just occasional grants from international non-profits—but her sense of connectedness at this point outweighs her economic insecurity.

When people live in a community that is on the move, there is a greater sense of belonging and optimism. In Santa Tecla, a small city only miles from San Salvador, when now-Vice President Oscar Ortiz was mayor, the crime rate in the urban core dropped dramatically. This has led to the growth of new restaurants and businesses and a far greater number of people out enjoying themselves in the evenings.

So what needs to be done to increase the chances for a good life for young Salvadorans as they come of age? The Salvadoran branch of the United Nations Development Program has been a strong advocate for the country and its residents to not only confront current problems but also to focus on the long-term well being of its citizens. This organization calls on government, and also other organizations and individuals, to focus on human development, the expanding of individuals' capabilities. Its report, *Informe sobre Desarrollo Humano El Salvador 2013: Imaginar Un Nuevo País. Hacerlo Posible* (Report on Human Development El Salvador 2013: Imagine a New Country. Make It Possible), proposes an emphasis on expanding the capabilities of people to broaden their options for advancement. This is seen as a two-fold process, first through skill development, enhanced education, and health promotion, and then through opening up more opportunities for individuals to exercise and develop these acquired capabilities, through work, civic participation, and other avenues. The report was directed not only to the Salvadoran government, but also to other donor nations, nongovernmental organizations, businesses, and individual Salvadorans. And there is much that these entities and individual citizens can do to help, in the broad areas of opportunities, pathways to opportunities, and guides and support.

Certainly, the actions and inactions of government have an impact on the opportunities that youth and young adults have. In the 2014 presidential elections in El Salvador, votes were split between a party of the right (ARENA) and a party of the left (FMLN). Centrist parties did not do well in the 2014 elections, and the hopes of some observers and Salvadorans that more moderate voices would emerge at this point in time are not being realized. Neither of the two presidential hopefuls mentioned the UNDP's report during their candidacy, and increased government attention on investing in the next generation does not seem likely after the results of the election. Salvador Sanchez Cerén of the left-wing party, the FMLN, won the 2014 presidential election by fewer than 7,000 votes, with 50.11% of the total vote. The candidate from the right-wing party claimed that there was fraud and called on the Army to intervene. Clearly the country remains bitterly divided.

However, some aspects of what needs to be done to better prepare youth for the future are not inherently liberal or conservative. A number of studies have demonstrated that committing resources to the development of the capabilities of people, especially during childhood and adolescence, brings a high rate of return on that investment to a society. An example of the benefits of spending on children and adolescents comes from a 50-country UNESCO study which found that increasing the average amount of schooling completed by one year could raise Gross Domestic Product (GDP) by 0.37% annually (El Salvador's GDP for the years 2010–2012 averaged less than 1.7%). But public spending on education in El Salvador remains low—between 2.8% and 3.6% of Gross Domestic Product (GDP) in 2008–2010.

Providing opportunities for employment for both gang members coming out of prison and would-be gang members also should be an area of common interest for all political parties and the business sector. If gang members and potential gang members do not see that there are alternative ways to make a living other than extortion, a solution to the problem of gangs is not possible.

What can other countries do to help Salvadorans coming of age? Both the European Union and individual countries in Europe contribute to and carry out development projects in El Salvador. The Partnership for Growth compact with El Salvador represents the largest U.S. concerted economic development program in the Western Hemisphere.

But while the U.S. provides substantial assistance to El Salvador, there is much more that it could do with and for El Salvador and other Latin American countries. The amount of foreign aid given by the U.S. to Latin America is small—less than $1.9 billion—and shrinking, from 10% of the foreign assistance budget in 2008 to 8% in 2012. While El Salvador receives more foreign aid than many other Latin American countries, the amount of support given to all Latin American countries is small in comparison to what the government spends on border security and immigration enforcement (nearly $18 billion in Fiscal Year 2012). This amount was almost 25% more than the funding for all other federal law enforcement agencies combined, including the FBI, Drug Enforcement Agency, and the Secret Service.

It is problematic to make a direct comparison between dollars spent in the U.S. on border enforcement and dollars granted in development aid—so that another country's individuals do not believe that they need to try to make it across that border to the United States. However, few would argue that there would be fewer Salvadorans attempting the long and dangerous journey through Guatemala and Mexico to the United States if they believed that they could have a good life in their home country.

Through programs and workshops that I have provided to Spanish-speaking parents in Wisconsin schools, I have worked and talked with many immigrants from Mexico and Central America in the past 20 years. The majority of these parents, who immigrated for a better life for their children, made a dangerous crossing to get to the United States. They come to a country with a language that most do not speak well, far away from families and friends. For those who settle in the Upper Midwest, it is a climate that is inhospitable in comparison with the sub-tropics (where I live in Wisconsin, the temperature did not get above freezing for the first 70 days of 2014). If they are undocumented, they "live in the shadows," going from home to work and back again, in fear of being deported. They left their home countries for the most part because they did not see opportunities there for themselves and for their children.

I brought in the accounts of three Salvadoran waiters in the "Stories" chapter in part to illustrate that having a decent job is a deterrent to migration. I asked each of them if they thought about going to the United States, and none were interested. Antonio said that perhaps he would be interested only if he could go legally, but he does not have close relatives in the U.S. who could arrange this. Toribio says he stays in El Salvador because his mother is there—and there he can surf year-round; it is too cold in the United States. The reply from José was: "The only important thing is to be close to family. Living there I would not know how my mother is, how my children are doing." In that oceanfront economy, they have found one of the places where there are family-supporting jobs. I review my interviews with the three waiters, all in their late 20s, and I see that they have managed to create the kind of stable and caring family that none of them had as children; they see staying close to family as the important thing in life. They each make enough money to get by, to acquire or be in the process of acquiring a small house, to be able to support their own families and, in two cases, their mothers. The push and pull of economic forces and the draw of *El Norte* are not sufficient to dislodge them.

Not only is it important to increase the number of areas in which opportunities are present, but there also needs to be a greater emphasis on *pathways* to opportunities. When the knowledge, skills, competencies, and abilities needed for success in a specific area are at least somewhat clear, young people will have a better idea of what they need to do to be successful. That is where the image of a pathway comes in. Youth have to be able to see the reasons for learning or mastering something and the necessary steps to do so—a feasible route to get from where they are to where they want to be.

In the "Education" chapter, I wrote about the disconnect between traditional university careers and the needs of the job market. If the universities were granted more flexibility in the programs of study and degrees that they offered and there was coordinated planning between the business sector, higher education, and in some cases non-profit organizations that provide training, this would result in more realistic options for youth that are more likely to lead to employment.

It is also essential to have knowledgeable guides. In the first chapter I stated that one of the characteristics of living between for youth in both developed and developing countries is that every generation can be seen as a separate country. However, the width of the generation gap is narrower if the parents' education level approximates that of the desired education of the youth. As Clayton Christensen and Henry Eyring have written, the experience of being a first-generation college student in the United States is like that of an athlete always playing away games—everything is unfamiliar all of the time. Salvadoran youth whose parents have at most a 5th-grade education can provide limited guidance to their children as to how best to prepare themselves and position themselves strategically in this rapidly changing world.

That is where non-profit organizations and volunteers can come in. An example of this is Glasswing,* a nonprofit organization that provides afterschool and other enrichment programs to school-age children and youth, largely through volunteers. The volunteers not only direct activities (like a chess club or environmental education projects) but through their informal contacts may be able to provide guidance to youth. Elisa, who appears in the "Stories" section, volunteered with Glasswing before starting to work with the organization. She told me about talking with one male who would

*Glasswing is one of two organizations (along with the Universidad Panamericana) that share in all the profits from this book.

be starting high school. In El Salvador, high school can be a more general 2-year program, which students planning on going straight to college take, or a more specialized 3-year program. This youth was planning on a 2-year program solely because a friend was planning on the 2-year option. However, given his interest in cooking, getting information about a 3–year program in the culinary arts was useful to him in deciding between high schools. Conversations with adults who are knowledgeable about schools can be valuable in situations such as this.

Programs like Glasswing connect adults who can be guides with youth, and it seems to me that there are also possibilities, through Skype and other technologies, for adults outside of El Salvador to serve as guides. I think of Salvadorans living abroad who could provide this mentorship to adolescents and young adults. Ex-Peace Corps Volunteers and others who had lived and worked in El Salvador could also serve in this way.

Tangible support, in the form of scholarships, can be instrumental for youth whose aspirations far exceed their resources. I chose Douglas's account of his life in the "Stories" chapter from among a number of cases of where youth had received scholarships and other help. Douglas had dropped out of school at age 14, worked construction for a year, and then was able to go back to school with a scholarship through his parish, donated from a church in the United States. It was not only the financial support but also the guidance from those in the parish that helped him enroll and then graduate from a premier university in El Salvador, the Universidad Centroamericana José Simeón Cañas. I also think of Melqui, a videographer/photographer with whom I have worked, who received his training through a scholarship to study briefly in the United States, and others whose scholarships have launched opportunities. I then wonder how many other talented and motivated Salvadorans remain "stuck" because of limited options and little support. One example of this comes from our study in Chalatenango of female recent high school graduates. One young woman was asked: "Given that your family can't afford to help you with college, what will you do?" Her answer (perhaps the least romantic statement on marriage I have ever heard) was: "Well, if I can't get a scholarship, I guess I'll get married."

As I think about young people coming of age, I am aware of the limitations of the term "pathway." I have used the phrase "liquid times" in this book as I think that it concisely communicates the rapidity with which things change. One implication of this is that the range of opportunities and the shape of the paths to reach them will change in the near future—and it will keep changing. Young people (and the rest of us) need to develop the habits of mind to engage in the kind of thinking where they can look for and analyze potential challenges and opportunities, and then take the steps to acquire additional skills or understanding to adapt to changing realities. They need to learn to be nimble, and this is another place where guides are essential.

So what will the future be like for those coming of age in El Salvador? The National Research Council report *Growing up Global* speaks to this:

> *While young people—a term used in this report to capture this phase of the life cycle roughly equivalent to the age range 10 to 24—have little opportunity to affect the speed and direction of change, some will soon be taking responsibility for its management as adults. Their success in making a well-timed and proficient transition from childhood to adulthood will fundamentally affect the extent to which they will be able to become active participants in and beneficiaries of global change in the future.*

When I read the phrase "some will soon be taking responsibility for its management as adults," I was reminded of a graduation speech that the American screenwriter and director (*The Avengers*) Joss Whedon gave at Wesleyan College in 2013. He referred to pessimism about the young being able to bring about changes this way:

> *So here's the thing about changing the world. It turns out that's not even the question, because you don't have a choice. You are going to change the world because that is actually*

what the world is. You do not pass through this life, it passes through you. You experience it, you interpret it, you act, and then it is different. That happens constantly. You are changing the world. You always have been....

Young people in El Salvador will change their country by the nature of their actions (and their inactions) in the coming years. It is very possible that they will be active in different forms than the older generations; an example of this is the use of social media for change described by Luís in the "Stories" chapter. Young Salvadorans do not join organizations (other than religious ones) in large numbers. Like the United States, in which half of those 18–30 consider themselves political independents, they are less attached to political parties than older Salvadorans.

There is an account of young people in Central America being nimble and inventive and saving their people, a myth that was told before the Spaniards came to this small part of the world. It is the story of Hunahpu and Xbalanque. This is my version of this story:

Hunahpu and Xbalanque, the twin heroes, are ready on the ball court for the game to begin. The game is ulama, played with a 9-pound ball. This game has been played in Central America and Mexico since the time that gods mingled with men. Think of soccer with a bigger, heavier ball, goals scored only when a player throws a deerskin-padded hip into an airborne or rolling ball, sending it into the goal. The game begins, and the twin teens are fast, daring, improvising.

This particular game is played in a ball court in the underworld, and the gods of the underworld of the Mayans were evil and vicious, preying on the humans who lived above. Hunahpu and Xbalanque had accepted their invitation to come to the underworld for the match, were on the lookout, but before the game started, a bat swooped down and cut off Hunahpú's head. The gods hung the head up in a ball court and challenged the twins to play ball with them.

Xbalanque found a turtle to sit on Hunahpú's shoulders in place of his head, and the game began. During the game, a rabbit near the court distracted the gods, and Xbalanque seized this opportunity to steal his brother's head from the wall and put it back in place. Much to the annoyance of the gods, the twins were now strong enough to tie the game. In their rage, the gods placed the twins in an oven and burned them until there was nothing left but ashes. And the gods stopped their gloating in wonder when the twins came back to life.

Before they had made their sojourn to the underworld, a magician had taught them how to die and come back from the dead. Impressed, the gods asked the twins to do the same for them. The brothers agreed, but after sacrificing the gods, they did not revive them. Having eliminated the gods of the underworld, Hunahpu and Xbalanque continued on their journeys.

Youth and young adults in El Salvador continue on their own journeys, with or without our support. How they make their way will affect their lives, their country, and ultimately, all of us.

Acknowledgments

The hardest thing about writing this is that I want to essentially put all those people and institutions that made this book possible at the front of the acknowledgements, and that is not possible. So the acknowledgements are in more or less a chronological order, starting with first coming to El Salvador and proceeding to the book's publication. I also know that I have forgotten to acknowledge some people, and for those that I neglected to name here, I apologize.

The powerful experiences as a Peace Corps Volunteer 1970-72 were what led me to want to return to El Salvador. For the hospitality of Don Mañuel Portillo España and his family and for my co-workers at Acción Comunitaria of the San Salvador municipality, and my supervisor Andrés Greogori, I am grateful, as well as for the support and friendship of Peace Corps Volunteers Marc Mihaly, Leslie Krebs and the late Allan Tesche and also the deceased Peace Corps Director Joseph Therrien.

I was fortunate that when I came to El Salvador as a Fulbright Scholar in 2005, I found in the Universidad Panamericana de El Salvador a welcoming institution. I have enjoyed the eight years I have worked with the chancellor Oscar Morán Folgar, vice-chancellors Nubia Adalila Mendoza Figueroa and Celina del Carmen López Urías, Robert Molina Castro, and many other administrators, faculty members, and staff. The Universidad Panamericana in 2005 was receptive to my research agenda related to migration, youth, and families. Virginia Quintana, a researcher employed there, also had an interest in this area, and together we have carried out seven studies, five in youth and migration, resulting in three monographs published in El Salvador and one in Spain. Funding from the NGO Carecen and the Heinrich Böll Foundation supported several of these research projects. Roberto Molina Castro. Without her collaboration and the support of the Universidad Panamericana, this book would not have come to be.

The University of Wisconsin-Whitewater was of great assistance in these research efforts. I made 14 trips to El Salvador between 2006 and 2013, and my home institution supported more than half of those. I received a publication grant which paid for much of the graphics work and also aid in the form of a paid internship for a student who was invaluable in the editing process. In addition to the fiscal backing, I appreciate the continual encouragement from my former Dean, Mary Pinkerton, and my current Dean, David Travis—the two best bosses I have had in my life. My colleagues in the Social Work Department have also been very supportive during this process.

I am grateful to the government of the United States. My Peace Corps service and the 2005 Fulbright award provided the opportunities and experience that led to this to this book. Additionally, support from the U.S. Embassy Cultural Affairs Office—Marjorie Stern, Stacy Session, and Fernando Herrera—allowed me to come to El Salvador in 2007 and 2008 to provide training to university faculty members, and I was also able to work on research projects during those trips.

There is a big difference between making a book possible and making a book better. I claim total responsibility for any inaccuracies in Coming of Age in El Salvador. Attempting to show the context in which youth become adults covers a lot of ground, some of it unfamiliar to me, and I apologize for any time when I did not get it right.

Getting it right does not necessarily mean getting it readable. In this book I am combining narrative and academic voices, and that has been difficult. I have been beyond fortunate in that the Director of the English Department's Professional Writing program, Janine Tobeck, invited me to have her Publication Development class work with an earlier version of this manuscript one semester and a later version in another semester. The feedback from both classes helped shape the form of the book. During an internship, RaeAnne Scargall's editing skills led to Coming of Age being far less clumsy than it otherwise would have been. Further (and immeasurable thanks) go to Dr. Tobeck, who on a volunteer basis spent many, many hours in the final edit.

I talked with many people about aspects of El Salvador for the book, and want to thank Eva Rodriguez, José Roberto Lopez, Luís Figueroa, Jesús Aguilar, Blanqui Alfaro, José William Garcia, Alejandro Dominguez, Denys Rodriguez, Mike Wise, Bryant Dwyer, Landon Loomis, Suzanne Kent, Laurie McGinley, Daniel Breneman, Tomás Guevara, Jaime Funes, David Hansen, Luís Romero, Oscar Isidro Miranda, Clayton Kennedy, Bri Erger, Kara Zucker, and Jed Byers. Staff at the Washington Office of Latin American assisted me in understanding concerns about organized crime in El Salvador.

I appreciate Danny Burridge giving me permission to use the story of Daniel in the "Stories" chapter. I want to thank those who read and reviewed parts and versions of the book. These include Kara Zucker, David McGee, Fritz McGough, Martiza Trejo, Karen Fisher, Eva Rodriguez, Luis Figueroa, Rita Richardson, Lavinia Tighe, Bert Kreitlow, and the students of UW-Whitewater's Publication Development courses in 2013 and 2014—Ethan Caliva, Ashley Dawson, Tia Dowding, Chris Greenwood, Dani Jason, Caitlin Johnson, Steven Kilger, Crystal Peterson, Ashley Pozel, Paulina Rieder, Nicole Roloff, RaeAnne Scargall, Melissa Champeau, Chris Fischer, Grant Francis, Ashley Hain, Missy Kennedy, Shia Lee, Tiffany Livick, Nikki Lutter, Rachel Nepper, Julia Teumer, and Shawna Webster.

Special thanks in reviewing go to Tim Muth, Mike Allison, and Joseph Wiltberger. They all know El Salvador well and raised important questions as well as reminding me of places where my information was incomplete. Parker Winship's comments and questions prodded me to make the writing clearer.

Melquisedec Escobar, a Salvadoran videographer and photographer, videotaped a number of the accounts in the "Stories" chapter, and he, Laurie McGinley, and David McGee gave me permission to use the photos used in the section breaks.

The cover design is by Jenny McGee (jennymcgeeart.com), and the internal book layout is by Kirsten Zimmer and Hope Winship. The layout of the photos in the section breaks and the chart in the "Living Between" chapter as well as the website (comingofagebook. com) are by Julie Esenther.

I have given credit individually to my wife Rita and my children Hope and Parker. I would wish that all people had a family as talented and supportive as the one I have.

And finally, I am grateful to the people of El Salvador, who have welcomed me again and again as I have lived in and visited your country. I would like to think that some of what makes Salvadorans so special has rubbed off on me over the years.

Appendix A—Remittances

Remittances (*remesas* in Spanish) are funds or other assets sent to their home country by migrants. Worldwide, remittance flows are over $400 billion a year and may reach $540 billion by 2016. Remittances account for a large share of the economy of many developing countries. In Tajikistan, the Kyrgyz Repubic, Nepal, and Lesotho, they make up more than 25% of these countries' Gross Domestic Product (GDP), the total economic activity of the country.

In El Salvador, in 2013, remittances sent from abroad totaled $3.97 billion dollars, a slight increase from 2012. This represents over 16% of the country's GDP. To put this in context, in the United States, manufacturing, retail sales, construction, and agriculture together almost reached 16% of the GDP.

The impact of remittances on Salvadoran life is wide reaching, and is covered in a number of chapters of this book. The growth of remittances from a negligible amount in 1980 to today's extent comes from the rapid growth in migration from El Salvador, as explained in the chapters "Past to Present" and "Migration." The ways in which remittances are tied to family relationships and communication in transnational families are described in the "Family" chapter. The impact of remittances on education is explained in the "Education" chapter, and the role of remittances in participation in the work force is covered in the "Economic Realities" chapter.

Over $4 billion a year is a lot of money, and economists, government officials and newspapers often bemoan the fact that families that receive remittances only save 1.4% of the money they receive, spending the remittances on housing, food, education, and other items. The point that the economists make is that money saved would then be available to lend for investment, leading to economic growth.

However, these critiques do not take into account the strained financial situations of the immigrants sending funds and the families receiving them. As 70% of those receiving remittances now have enough resources not to be in poverty, and the remittances that families receive are typically in the $150–$200 range, there is often little money left over after paying for the necessities. Expecting poor Salvadorans to fuel economic development through savings is not realistic.

Appendix B—United States Immigration Laws

I am including this brief appendix because many people in the United States have an incomplete knowledge of U.S. immigration laws and procedures. Understanding Salvadoran immigration to the U.S. is easier with more information on what the realistic options are for potential immigrants. Readers who want more information on immigration issues can find this at the Migration Policy Institute (migrationpolicy.org), the Pew Hispanic Center (pewhispanic.org), and the American Immigration Council (immigrationpolicy.org).

As with any book that deals with current events, aspects of this will become outdated as events happen. It is my hope that some of the material on immigration laws will no longer be current if the U.S. Congress passes some measure of immigration reform legislation.

Over the last 50 years, the number of immigrants to the United States has reached levels not seen since the early years of the 20th century; at present, a little more than 1 out of every 7 persons in the U.S. was born elsewhere. Salvadorans are a part of that migration. In this appendix, I want to put current migration in a historical context, show how current legislation came to be, and answer several commonly asked questions about immigration to the U.S.

There have been four periods in which mass immigration has occurred in the United States. The first, predating the nation's birth, was during the settling of the original colonies in the 1600s and 1700s. The second coincided with westward expansion in the mid-19th century. The population of the United States was only 38.6 million in 1870, and in the 50 years that followed, 26.2 million persons immigrated to the United States. Almost all were from Europe, but in the early 1900s more were from Eastern Europe and Italy than from Germany, England, and Scandinavia, as earlier. As more immigrants were Jewish and Roman Catholic, concern grew among Protestants, the dominant religion at the time, about the changing face of the country.

Legislation passed in the early 20th century was in many ways racially-based and demonstrated an unwillingness to accept other cultures. The 1917 Immigration Act prohibited immigration from a newly drawn "Asiatic barred zone" which included most of Southeast Asia, British India, and almost all of the Middle East. A total of no more than 150,000 immigrants a year and a national-origins quota system were part of The Immigration and Naturalization Act of 1924. There was a ceiling on the number of immigrants who could be admitted to the United States from each country, based on the proportion of the U.S. population in 1870—before the large-scale immigration.

The national-origins quota system was maintained in the 1952 Immigration and Nationality Act, but the total ban on immigrants from Asian countries was lifted. The 1965 Immigration Act did away with national-origins quotas and established family reunification and needed skills as the primary criteria for immigration. This law also did away with the temporary worker program, commonly referred to as the Bracero program. When this law went into effect in 1968, the approximately 1 million largely Mexican workers who had been coming in for months at a time to pick crops and work in other parts of farming had no option other than to cross the borders illegally.

By the mid-1980s, there were between 3 and 5 million unauthorized immigrants in the United States. To address the issue of illegal immigration, Congress passed the Immigration Reform and Control Act of 1986 (IRCA), which increased border enhancement, established penalties for employers who employed unauthorized immigrants, and granted legal status to unauthorized immigrants who had lived in the U.S. for a minimum of 5 years. Many of the Salvadorans 50 years and older living legally in the United States came to the U.S. during the war and then were able to get permanent residency through IRCA, and many later became citizens.

The extent of unauthorized immigration did not decrease due to the IRCA, but rather increased in the 1990s. The combination of stagnant economies in Mexico and Central America in the 1990s and the economic boom in the United States during that time propelled this surge of migration.

There was a strong possibility in 2000 and 2001 that there would be a temporary worker program and other immigration reforms. President George W. Bush and Mexican President Vicente Fox were in the process of discussing this, but the terrorist acts of September 11, 2011 ended any hope of immigration reform at that time.

At present there are approximately 11 million persons in the United States without legal authorization. This compares to the 18 million immigrants who are naturalized citizens and 11 million who are legal permanent or temporary residents.

Among the legal temporary residents is the category of Temporary Protected Status (TPS). If the United States designates a country for TPS due to conflicts such as civil war or environmental disasters, individuals are eligible to apply to come to the U.S. and can work legally. However, there is no direct path from TPS to legal permanent residency or citizenship. El Salvador became eligible for TPS after the earthquakes in 2001. More than 275,000 Salvadorans have participated in TPS, and a large number who have been working legally in the U.S. under TPS since the early 2000s.

People often ask: "Why don't illegal immigrants just apply and come here legally?" They are unaware that most green cards are reserved for legal permanent residents or high-skilled jobs. An employer can request permission to bring in a qualified foreign worker if they cannot find a qualified U.S. worker first. This applies mostly to scientists or other professionals.

Parents of Salvadoran youth who have become citizens can petition to bring their children to the United States legally—they would become legal permanent residents. However, there is such a backlog of applications that the wait can be 5 to 10 years for the application to be granted.

To be able to live legally in the U.S., there are also the related categories of refugees and asylees. Refugees are persons from another country who are admitted to the U.S. when it is determined that due to a "well-founded fear of persecution"—based on "race, religion, membership in a particular social group, political opinion, or national origin," they would be harmed if they returned to their home country. Asylees petition for asylum once they arrive in the U.S. based on the same criteria as refugees. The criteria for determining refugee and asylum status are at times political. During the Salvadoran civil war, persons fleeing El Salvador for fear of the right-wing death squads were not granted refugee status.

While the vast majority of the 11 million undocumented immigrants "live in the shadows" in fear of deportation, 1.76 million young people have temporary legal status (at least until the U.S.

presidential elections in 2016) through the Deferred Action for Childhood Arrivals (DACA) program. President Obama created the DACA program through an Executive Order in June 2012. Applicants must have arrived in the U.S. before they turned 16, be younger than 31 now, be high school graduates or in school, or have served in the military. This program gives young people who are approved for this the ability to work legally in the United States.

What does the term "illegal immigrant" mean? The phrase has both literal and highly symbolic meanings. In legal terms in the United States, entering the country without permission is a misdemeanor criminal offense. In many states, getting a speeding ticket is also a misdemeanor criminal offense. I tell people "Don't call unauthorized immigrants 'illegals' unless you are also willing to refer to yourself that way if you have ever gotten a speeding ticket."

However, the status of being here without legal authorization has implications both legal and also for one's sense of identity. The legal implications are many. Since the passage of the Real ID Law of 2005, individuals who are undocumented cannot get driver's licenses (although very recently some cities and states are starting to issue a quasi-license or permit). The lack of a legal driver's license means that immigrants who need to drive to work or take their children to school do so in fear of being stopped.

One can be deported, and while the emphasis in the Obama administration has been on deporting criminals, two-thirds of the nearly 2 million deportation cases involve people who had committed minor infractions, including traffic violations (e.g. driving without a valid driver's license), or had no criminal record at all.

There are also other implications for those who are undocumented. Consider the situation of an undocumented Salvadoran woman who has lived and worked in the United States for almost 20 years. She is a good worker, a good mother, and active in her congregation. Yet she feels a sense of social exclusion, in that her immigration status separates her in many ways from a country of which she feels very much a part.

After decades of immigration, unauthorized immigrants are woven into American society, including a substantial number of families with "mixed status." Over 9 million families have at least one unauthorized adult and one U.S.-born child.

Notes

Chapter 1: Living Between

5   Education statistics from Lindo-Fuentes (2008).

Information on young women's plans from Ramos (2011), p. 137.

6   Information on ages of first marriages from http://www.infoplease. com/ipa/A0005061.html from U.S. Census.gov and http://www. quandl.com/demography/age-at-first-marriage-female-all-countries.

8   Facebook statistics from www.internetworldstats.com/central.htm.

In 2012, when the number of murders dropped sharply, El Salvador was still ranked 44th (out of 120 countries). See Interpeace (2013).

The *Economist* article "The Lottery of Life" listed Switzerland, Australia, and Norway as the three best places to be born. The United States and Germany were tied for 16th (see http://www.economist. com/news/21566430-where-be-born-2013-lottery-life).

9   Figures for the four countries come from The United Nations Development Program's 2011 Human Development Report, *Sustainability and Equity: A Better Future for All*. The United Nations compiles a Human Development Index (HDI), a composite statistic of life expectancy, education, and income data that ranks 187 countries (low is good). The HDI ranking for the United States was 4, for Argentina was 45, for El Salvador 105, and for Uganda 161.

For information on the Gallup study on happiness and perceived well-being, see Clifton (2012).

Phone interview with Elena Löber, August 23, 2013.

Interview with Oscar, the owner of a number of small businesses on the coast of El Salvador, May 26, 2013.

11   Interview with Raúl, a musician and audio technician who had lived in Southern California for almost a decade before returning on May 23, 2013.

Chapter 2: Geography

17 Gabriela Mistral's "El Salvador" appeared in *Repertorio Americano* XXVII: 9 (1933, September 2).

18 Story of the hike to El Higueral used by permission from Clayton Kennedy, from the blog he had during his Peace Corps years: http://claykennedy.wordpress.com/.

20 For photos of the beauty of El Salvador, see http://goo.gl/qk7ndo.

Information on Hurricane Mitch from the National Oceanic and Atmospheric Association (2009). Information on Hurricane Stan from http://weather.wikia.com/wiki/Hurricane_Stan.

21 Information on Hurricane Ida and Tropical Depression 12-E from www.nytimes.com/2009/11/09/world/americas/09salvador.html?_r=0; http://www.huffingtonpost.com/2009/11/13/hurricane-ida-hits-el-sal_n_357725.html; and http://reliefweb.int/report/el-salvador/tropical-depression-12-e-emergency-appeal-n%C2%B0-mdrsv004-preliminary-final-report.

Information on El Salvador's soil composition, earthquakes, and landslides from Bommer, et al. (2002). Information on the 2013 San Miguel volcano from Ministerio de Medio Ambiente y Recursos Naturales http://www.marn.gob.sv and Tim Muth's *Tim's El Salvador Blog*, http://luterano.blogspot.com (2013, December 19). Information on the 2005 Santa Ana volcano from correspondence with José Roberto Lopez, active in the watershed governance for this region, July 15, 2013. One can monitor volcanic activity at http://www.volcanodiscovery.com/el-salvador.html. For speculation on the volcanic root of the Dark Ages, see Wohletz (2000).

23 Tegel's article also elaborates on the impact of climate change. See http://www.globalpost.com/dispatch/news/regions/americas/120714/el-salvador-climate-change-rising-sea-level.

For the World Risk Index information see United Nations University (2012).

24 Studies in which youth did not mention environmental precariousness when asked about their major concerns include Ramos (2011) and Santacruz Giralt & Carranza (2009).

Chapter 3: Past to Present

25 Unless otherwise noted, material on Salvadoran history came from Ching (2013), Byrne (1996), Arnson (1982), and Boland (2001).

27 On the *Matanza*, see Anderson (2001) and Gould & Lauria-Santiago (2008).

Percentages of land held by groups from Byrne (1996), p. 20.

29 On the role of ORDEN, see United States Bureau of Citizenship and Immigration Services (2000).

For information on the protests of the Miss Universe pageant, see Brockett (2005), p. 77.

31 On Robert White's testimony, see Nordland (1984) and http://www.derechos.org/nizkor/salvador/doc/white.html.

32 For a transcript of Reagan's televised "Address to the Nation on United States Policy in Central America," 9 May 1984, see http://www.reagan.utexas.edu/archives/speeches/1984/50984h.htm.

33 On senior officers collecting pay from nonexistent soldiers, see Byrne (1996), p. 79.

34 On the end of the war, see Binford (2002). On the UN assessment of a "negotiated revolution," see Byrne (1996), p. 193.

35 Binford (2002), p. 205. For the Truth Commission's report, see United Nations Security Council (1993).

36 For more on post-2000 politics in El Salvador, see Perla (2013).

Information about the campaign ad from Rubin (2004).

37 On the 2009 election, see "Left Turn: El Salvador's Presidential Election" (2009).

Chapter 5: Family

84 Saskia Sassen summarized in Parreñas (2005), p. 146.

85   Census data from Dirección General de Estadística y Censos (2008). Survey information from Ramos (2011), p. 146.

86   Quotation from Abrego (2009). For more of Abrego's work, see: Menjivar, C. and Abrego, L. (2009). "Parents and Children across Borders: Legal Instability and Intergenerational Relations in Guatemalan and Salvadoran Families. In N. Foner (Ed.), *Across Generations: Immigrant Families in America* (160–189). New York: New York University Press; Abrego, L. (2009). Economic Well-Being in Salvadoran Transnational Families: How Gender Affects Remittance Practices. *Journal of Marriage and Family, 71*(4), 1070–1085; and Abrego, L. (2014). *Sacrificing Families: Navigating Laws, Labor, and Love across Borders*. Stanford, CA: Stanford University Press.

88   Quotations from Parreñas (2005), p. 156.

90   Interview with Bri Erger, Peace Corps Volunteer, in Ataco, El Salvador, January 13, 2012.

92   Conversation with Sonia Nazario, November 28, 2011.

94   Parent respondent quoted in Rojas-Flores et al. (2013), p. 278.

95   Ramos' (2011) survey results from p. 92.

96   Levine and Dean (2012) and Gould are quoted in Khrais (2012).

97   Santacruz Giralt and Carranza's (2009) survey results from p. 36. Interview with Dr. Candelaria Navas, June 26, 2012.

98   For research on happiness, see Leung et al. (2011), and Holder & Coleman (2009).

Chapter 6: Migration

100 Quotation from de Blij (2010), p. 3.

Information on Latino population in the U.S. from Hispanic Population Trends, at http://www.pewhispanic.org/2013/02/15/hispanic-population-trends/ph_13-01-23_ss_hispanics5/. As of

2011 data, there were 33,539,000 Mexicans, 1,952,000 Salvadorans, 1,889,000 Cubans, and 1,528,000 Dominicans. U.S. emigration data cited in Mark Rice's "Not Everyone Wants to Live in America" (2010). See http://www.forbes.com/2010/06/04/immigration-emigration-expats-opinions-contributors-mark-rice.html. For El Salvador's 2007 census data, see Dirección General de Estadística y Censos (2008).

Quotation from S. Kent (2010), p. 74.

101 For more on social capital, see Dekker & Uslaner (2001).

Quotation from de Blij (2010), p. 6.

On the numbers of Salvadorans in U.S. cities, see http://mediacenter.laprensagrafica.com/infografias/i/eua-el-pais-con-mas-salvadorenos-en-el-mundo.

102 Interview with Leonor Guerra, Deputy Director of Huertas Elementary School, City of Ilobasco, October 14, 2005.

For more on the Vice Ministry for El Salvadorans Living Abroad, see Marcin (2013).

103 Survey data from Ramos (2011) is from p. 141.

104 Quotation from the UNDP report (2005), p. 4.

105 For more information on our focus group, see Quintana & Winship (2010).

Amnesty International's Annual Report 2012 can be found at http://www.amnesty.org/en/region/mexico/report-2012, and the COFAMIDE numbers are reported in Ayala (2012).

106 For more on the dangers of "The Beast," see Penhaul (2010). Nazario's interview (in Macabasco, 2006) can be found at http://www.motherjones.com/politics/2006/03/train-death?page=2. Zoila Figueroa's story is recorded in Pearson (2013, April 9), at http://www.nydailynews.com/new-york/citizenship-now/pregnant-woman-kidnapped-tortured-immigrating-u-s-article-1.1312307#ixzz-2Rm8cbWUE.

107 Deportation figures from the *New York Times'* Editorial Board's opinion piece "Not One More" (2013, October 27). See http://www.nytimes.com/2013/10/28/opinion/not-one-more.html?_r=0.

Interview with José William Garcia, October 13, 2005.

Chapter 7: Education

109 Interview with Andrés Dominguez, June 12, 2012.

112 On the historical overview of education in El Salvador, see Lindo-Fuentes (2008) and Dewees et al. (1994).

113 Information about the *Plan Social Educativo* (PSE) is quoted in Mills (2012).

114 2013 data on remittance amounts from "Crecen Remesas de Salvadoreños en EE.UU." Figures on use of remittances from López, K. (2011).

National Bureau of Economic Research data from Cos & Ureta (2003).

World Bank study information from Acosta (2006).

115 Educational quality concerns are described in the United Nations Development Program's (2013) *Informe sobre Desarrollo Humano El Salvador 2013.*

Comparative GDP data from Bertelsmann Stiftung (2012).

Data from the 2012 study on teacher training is from SITEAL (2012).

Interview with Luis Monterrosa, June 15, 2012.

116 On the length of school days, see 1995 reforms in Lindo-Fuentes (2008). The teacher speaking about tiredness is quoted in PNUD (2013), p. 148: "Lo que uno piensa es: 'Las tardes no sirven'. Pero no es que no sirvan, porque los cipotes vienen a aprender, sino que uno ya va cansado. Yo, aquí, llego arrastrándome" (translation mine).

117 For average length of schooling, see Dirección General de Estadística y Censos (2012).

On the importance of a "culture of reading" for student achievement, see Daniels & Steres (2011). The "why are you reading?" conversation was shared with me by Bri Eggers, January 14, 2012.

Interview with Dr. Hector Samour, June 15, 2012.

118 United Nations Population Fund information cited in Morán (2013).

Data on contraception rates is from M. M. Kent (2010).

119 Information about the UES during the civil war comes from the United Nations Security Council (1993).

120 Teacher quotation from United Nations Development Program (2013), p. 163: "Yo, como maestro, no lo estoy preparando para que él vea sus cualidades, vea sus potencialidades, vea sus posibilidades [...] No lo estamos preparando para que él vea una gestión de su conocimiento, de lo que él conoce, de las habilidades y, con base en eso, genere una situación productive. Estos programas ya no sirven, hay que capacitor a los profesores en cosas nuevas." (Translation mine.)

Oscar Carlos Picardo is quoted in Saunders et al. (2012), p. 8. The same report includes graduation rates (p. 9).

121 Marco Penado of Manpower El Salvador is quoted in the blog *Voices on the Border* (2011).

Interview with Dr. Hector Samour, June 15, 2012.

Chapter 8: Economic Realities

125 On neoliberal policy shifts and the currency conversion of *colones* to dollars, see Seelke (2012). Quotation is from p. 10.

Information on foreign capital and constraints on the El Salvadoran economy from Joint United States Government–Government of El Salvador Technical Team (2011).

126 Acevedo's estimate of the cost of violence is on p. 79 of the Joint United States Government–Government of El Salvador Technical Team's (2011) report. Percentage of businesses citing violence as a hindrance to their functioning is on p. 74.

127 Coca-Cola quotation from Quintana & Winship (2010).

129 The study for the PRISMA Foundation was authored by Kandel & Cuéllar (2011).

130 Information on formal/informal labor in the U.S. from Nightingale and Wandner (2011). On employment in the informal sector in El Salvador, see Dirección General de Estadística y Censos (2012).

Census data from Dirección General de Estadística y Censos (2012).

131 Minimum wage information from "Funes avala decretos para el aumento al salario mínimo" (2013).

132 Average income data are available from the World Bank (2014).

Income distribution in El Salvador available from Index Mundi (2009).

Gini Index information for El Salvador from UNDP (2013), and, for the U.S., from "Gini in the Bottle" (2013).

133 For the *New York Times* interview of Ricardo Poma, see Garfinkel (2010).

Figures on growing inequality are from Byrne (1996).

Data on poverty rates measured by CBAs and on household amenities are from the Dirección General de Estadística y Censos (2008).

136 See Muth (2010) for more on fast food chains and remittances.

137 On percentages of youth employed, by gender, see UNDP (2013), p. 176.

On *ninis*, see López, T. (2012).

138 Survey responses from Ramos (2011), p. 35. Figures on education levels of the unemployed from Saunders et al. (2012).

Conversations with Mike Wise on June 6 and June 8, 2012.

Conversation with Roberto Molina Castro, General Secretary of the Universidad Panamericana, about engineering graduates getting jobs in the 1960s, June 11, 2012. Conversation with Andrés Dominguez August 3, 2013.

139 The United Nations Economic Commission for Latin America and the Caribbean is quoted in S. Kent (2010), p. 166.

Conversation with Luís Romero September 16, 2005.

140 For more on the Millennium Challenge Corporation's El Salvador Compact, see http://www.mcc.gov/pages/countries/overview/el-salvador. Quotation on the Partnership for Growth program from Embassy of the United States, El Salvador (2011).

Chapter 9: Violence

144 On violence ranking and the 2012 drop in homicides, see Fox (2013).

For Lonely Planet's reassurance to travelers, see http://www.lonely-planet.com/el-salvador/practical-information/health. El Salvador made Lonely Planet's Top Ten Countries to Visit list in 2010. For the *Telegraph*'s travel recommendation, see http://www.telegraph.co.uk/travel/destinations/centralamericaandcaribbean/10539345/Twenty-destinations-for-2014-El-Salvador.html.

145 For information on conviction rates, see United States Department of State (2011).

Data on per capita murder rates available from the United Nations Office on Drugs and Crime (2014).

146 On increased violence in rural areas, see Garzon (2013). Also see *Tim's El Salvador Blog* (Muth, 2013, July 18) for analysis of the data. On rising insecurities about violence, see Ramsey (2012).

On estimates of gang numbers, see Santos (2013).

147 Conversation in Suchitoto on August 17, 2005.

148 Information on the government response to gang growth from Arana (2005) and Fariña et al. (2010).

149 On Funes's use of the army, see Herrmann (2012).

Data on per capita homicides available from the United Nations Office on Drugs and Crime (2014). Information about murder rates dropping after the gang truce of 2012 from "Central American murder rates remain same to slightly lower" (2014).

149 On the impact on gangs of prison segregation and uniforms, see Looft (2012). Excellent reporting on gangs and narco-trafficking throughout Latin American comes from InSight Crime, a project of Fundacion Ideas para la Paz (FIP) in Bogota, Colombia, with funding from the Open Society Foundations. American University's Center for Latin American and Latino Studies (CLALS) is a sponsor of and additional host to the project.

150 On the lack of investment in social services, education, and job training, see Fariña et al. (2010), p. 23.

151 On extortion and the case of bus drivers, see Parkinson (2014).

Interview with Mauricio Aracón, March 30, 2012.

153 On the doubling of cocaine seized, see Cawley (2013).

For statistics on ages of the majority of homicide victims, see Fox (2013). Survey responses on top concerns from Ramos (2011), pp. 128–129.

154 Numbers of students and teachers killed as reported in Catholic Online (2012).

155 See Santacruz Giralt and Carranza (2009), p. 116.

Chapter 10: Looking toward the Future

159 On the problematic job outlook for young adults in Europe, see Weardon (2013). Ye Zhihong quoted in Bradsher (2013).

161 See Santacruz Giralt and Carranza (2009), p. 46.

162 On the role of spirituality and religious coping, see Salas-Wright, Olate, & Vaughn (2013). Religious coping refers to connections with religious communities and religious practices as ways of managing stressful life events. Spirituality, or connection or relationship between a person and God (or some Transcendence like a Greater Power), may or may not be linked to religious communities or practices. See Kozol (2000), pp. 4–5.

166 El Salvador's GDP data from Index Mundi (2013).

166 Data on U.S. spending on foreign aid and border security from Meyer & Sullivan (2012) and Meissner et al. (2013).

170 Quote from National Research Council (2005), p. 17.

Appendix A: Remittances

177 Data on remittances from Ratha et al. (2013), pp. 1 and 5. The latest data and resources on remittances are available from the World Bank at http://www.worldbank.org/migration.

El Salvador remittance figures for 2013 from "El Salvador recibe $3.969 millones en remesas familiares." United States figures from United States Department of Commerce, Bureau of Economic Analysis (2014).

178 For analysis of remittances as a source of development, see: Ratha, D. (2003). Workers' Remittances: An Important and Stable source of External Development Finance. *Global Development Finance 2003: Striving for Stability in Development Finance* (pp. 157–175). Washington, DC: International Monetary Fund; Terry, D. F. & Wilson, S. R. (Eds.). (2005). *Beyond Small Change: Making Migrant Remittances Count.* Washington, DC: Inter-American Development Bank; and Jones, R. C. (1998). Remittances and Inequality: A Question of Migration Stage and Geographic Scale. *Economic Geography 74*(1): 8–25.

Appendix B: United States Immigration Laws

179 Material on early immigration to the U.S. is from Gerber, D. (2013). *American Immigration: A Very Short Introduction.* Oxford and New York: Oxford University Press; and Takaki, R. (2008). *Strangers from a Different Shore: A History of Multicultural America* (1st Rev. Ed.). New York: Back Bay Books.

180 On the IRCA and interrupted reforms of the early 2000s, see Hipsman & Meissner (2013).

181 For information on Temporary Protected Status, see http://www.uscis.gov/humanitarian/temporary-protected-status-deferred-enforced-departure/temporary-protected-status.

181 For details on why more immigrants don't simply apply for legal status, see Immigration Policy Center (2013).

On refugee and asylum status, see http://www.uscis.gov/humanitarian/refugees-asylum.

182 On DACA, see http://www.uscis.gov/humanitarian/consideration-deferred-action-childhood-arrivals-process.

On deportations under the Obama administration, see Thompson & Cohen (2014).

For a portrait of our immigrant nation, see Pew Research Hispanic Trends Project (2013).

References

Abrego, L. (2009). Rethinking El Salvador's transnational families. [Special Issue]. *NACLA Report on the Americas* 42(6), 28–32.

Acosta, P. (2006). *Labor supply, school attendance, and remittances from international migration: The case of El Salvador.* World Bank Policy Research Working Paper 3903. World Bank. doi: <u>10.1596/1813-9450-3903</u>

American Psychological Association. (nd). Understanding chronic stress. Retrieved from <u>http://www.apa.org/helpcenter/understanding-chronic-stress.aspx</u>

Amnesty International (2012). *Annual report 2012: Mexico.* Retrieved from <u>http://www.amnesty.org/en/region/mexico/report-2012</u>

Anderson, T. P. (2001). *Matanza: The 1932 slaughter that traumatized a nation, shaping U.S. Salvadoran policy to this day* (2nd ed.). Willimantic, CT: Curbstone Press.

Appadurai, A. (2008). Global ethnoscapes: Notes and queries for a transnational anthropology. In S. Khagram and P. Levitt (Eds.), *The transnational studies reader: Intersections and innovations* (pp. 50–63). New York: Routledge.

Arana, A. (2005, May/June). How the street gangs took Latin America. *Foreign Affairs.* Retrieved from <u>http://www.foreignaffairs.com/articles/60803/ana-arana/how-the-street-gangs-took-central-america</u>

Armstrong, R., & Shenk, J. (1972). *El Salvador: The face of revolution.* Boston: South End Press.

Arnett, J. J. (2011). Emerging adulthood(s): The cultural psychology of a new life stage. In L. A. Jensen (Ed.), *Bridging cultural and developmental psychology: New syntheses in theory, research, and policy* (pp. 255–275). New York: Oxford University Press.

Arnson, C. (1982). *El Salvador: A revolution confronts the United States.* Washington, DC: Institute for Policy Studies.

Ayala, E. (2012, May 17). Protection for Salvadoran migrants en route to U.S. Retrieved from http://www.ipsnews.net/2012/05/protection-for-salvadoran-migrants-en-route-to-u-s-3/31/

Bauman, Z. (2006). *Liquid times: Living in an age of uncertainty.* New York: John Wiley and Sons.

BBC News. (2011, September 16). Belize and El Salvador added to US drug blacklist. Retrieved from http://www.bbc.co.uk/news/world-latin-america-14941749

Benitez, J. L. (2011). *La comunicación transnacional de las e-familias migrantes.* San Salvador: United Nations Development Program and the Universidad Centroamericano "José Simeon Cañas."

Benokraitis, N. V. (2008). *Marriages and families: Changes, choices, and constraints* (6th ed.). Upper Saddle River, NJ: Pearson Prentice Hall.

Bertelsmann Stiftung. (2012). BTI 2012—El Salvador country report. Gütersloh: Author. Retrieved from api.gobiernoabierto.gob.sv/attachments/205/download

Binford, L. (2002). Violence in El Salvador: A rejoinder to Phillippe Bourgois' "The Power of Violence in War and Peace." *Ethnography, 3*(2), 201–219. doi: 10.1177/1466138102003002004

Boff, L., & Boff, C. (1987). *Introducing liberation theology* (p. 7). Maryknoll, NY: Orbis Books.

Boland, R. (2001). *Culture and customs of El Salvador.* Westport, CT: Greenwood Press.

Bommer, J. J., Bénito, B., Ciudad-Real, M., Lemoine, A., López Menjívar, M., Madariaga, R., ... & Rosa, H. (2002). The El Salvador earthquakes of January and February 2001: Context, characteristics, and implications for seismic risk. *Soil Dynamics and Earthquake Engineering, 22*(5). 389–418. doi: 10.1016/S0267-7261(02)00024-6

Bradsher, K. (2013, January 24). Chinese graduates say no thanks to factory jobs. *The New York Times*. Retrieved from http://www.nytimes.com/2013/01/25/business/as-graduates-rise-in-china-office-jobs-fail-to-keep-up.html?_r=2&

Brenneman, R. (2011). *Homies and hermanos: God and gangs in Central America*. Oxford: Oxford University Press.

Brenneman, R. (2013). *Perquin musings: A gringo's journey in El Salvador*. Available from http://www.amazon.com/PERQU-N-MUS-INGS-gringo-s-journey-salvador-ebook/dp/B00C559Z54/ref=tmm_kin_swatch_0?_encoding=UTF8&sr=&qid=

Brockett, C. D. (2005). *Political movements and violence in Central America* (p. 77). Boston: Cambridge University Press.

Brown, B. B., Larson, R. W., & Saraswathi, T. T. (Eds.). (2002). *The world's youth: Adolescence in eight regions of the globe* (p. 2). Cambridge and New York: Cambridge University Press.

Byrne, H. (1996). *El Salvador's civil war: A study in revolution*. Boulder, CO: Lynne Rienner Publishers.

Catholic Online. (2012, March 13). El Salvador students, teachers fall prey to extortion, muggings and murder. *Catholic Online*. Retrieved from http://www.catholic.org/news/international/americas/story.php?id=45193

Cawley, M. (2013, December 18). El Salvador gangs getting deeper into drug trafficking: Police. *InSight Crime*. Retrieved from http://archive-org.com/page/3544465/2014-01-16/http://www.insightcrime.org/news-briefs/el-salvador-gangs-deepening-drug-trafficking-involvement-police

Central American murder rates remain same to slightly lower. (2014, January 24). Weblog. Central American Politics. Retrieved from http://centralamericanpolitics.blogspot.com/2014/01/central-american-murder-rates-remain.html

Ching, E. (2013). *Authoritarian El Salvador: Politics and the origins of the military regimes, 1880–1940.* South Bend, IN: University of Notre Dame Press.

Christensen, C. M., & Eyring, H. J. (2011). *The innovative university: Changing the DNA of higher education from the inside out.* San Francisco: Jossey-Bass.

Clifton, J. (2012, December 19). Latin Americans most positive in the world. *Gallup World.* Retrieved from http://www.gallup.com/poll/159254/latin-americans-positive-world.aspx

CONARE (National Council of University Chancellors of Costa Rica). (2011). *Programa estado de la nación en desarrollo humano sostenible (Summary of the state of the region on sustainable human development).* San José, Costa Rica: PEN.

Cos, A., & Ureta, M. (2003). *International migration, remittances, and schooling: Evidence from El Salvador.* Cambridge, MA: National Bureau of Economic Research, Working Paper 9766. Retrieved from http://www.nber.org/papers/w9766

Crecen remesas de salvadoreños en EE.UU. (2014, January 19). *El Tiempo Latino.* Retrieved from http://eltiempolatino.com/news/2014/jan/19/crecen-remesas-de-salvadorenos-en-eeuu/

Daniels, E., & Steres, M. (2011). Examining the effects of a school-wide reading culture on the engagement of middle school students. *Research in Middle Level Education 35*(2), 1–13. Retrieved from http://www.amle.org/BrowsebyTopic/WhatsNew/WNDet.aspx?ArtMID=888&ArticleID=43

Danner, M. (1993). *The massacre at El Mozote.* New York: Random House Vintage Books.

De Blij, H. (2010). *The power of place: Geography, destiny, and globalization's rough landscape.* New York: Oxford University Press.

Dekker, P., & Uslaner, E. M. (2001). *Social capital and participation in everyday life.* New York: Routledge.

Dewees, A., Evans, E., King, C., & Shiefelbein, E. (1994). *Educación básica y parvularia. Diagnóstico del sistema de desarrollo de recursos humanos de El Salvador.* San Salvador: Harvard Institute for International Development, Fundación Empresarial para el Desarrollo Educativo (El Salvador) y Universidad Centroamericana "José Simeón Cañas."

Diener, E., Ng, W., Harter, J., & Arora, R. (2010). Wealth and happiness across the world: Material prosperity predicts life evaluation, whereas psychosocial prosperity predicts positive feeling. *Journal of Personality and Social Psychology, 99*(1), 52–61.

Dirección General de Estadística y Censos. (2008). *VI Censo de Población y Vivienda 2007.* San Salvador, El Salvador: Author.

Dirección General de Estadística y Censos. (2012). *Encuesta de hogares de propósitos multiples 2012.* San Salvador, El Salvador: Author.

Dreby, J. (2009). Negotiating work and parenting over the life course. In N. Foner (Ed.), *Across generations: Immigrant families in America* (pp. 190–218). New York: New York University Press.

Editorial Board. (2013, October 27). Not one more. *The New York Times.* Retrieved from http://www.nytimes.com/2013/10/28/opinion/not-one-more.html?_r=0

El Salvador recibe $3.969 millones en remesas familiares. (2014, January 23). *La Prensa Grafica.* Retrieved from http://www.laprensagrafica.com/2014/01/23/el-salvador-recibe-3969-millones-en-remesas-familiares

Embassy of the United States, El Salvador. (2011, September 20). FOMILENIO celebrates 4 year anniversary. Retrieved from http://sansalvador.usembassy.gov/news/2011/09/15.html

Fariña, L. P., Miller, S., & Cavallaro, J. L. (2010). *No place to hide: Gang, state, and clandestine violence in El Salvador.* Cambridge, MA: Harvard Law School, Harvard University.

Fox, E. (2013, January 4). El Salvador homicides fell over 40% in 2012. Retrieved from http://www.insightcrime.org/news-briefs/el-salvador-homicides-fell-over-40-percent-2012

Freire, P. (1970). *Pedagogy of the oppressed*. New York: Herder and Herder.

Friedman, M. (1962). *Capitalism and freedom* (p. 86). Chicago: University of Chicago Press.

Funes avala decretos para el aumento al salario mínimo. (2013, July 3). elsalvador.com. Retrieved from http://www.elsalvador.com/mwedh/nota/nota_completa.asp?idCat=47673&idArt=8012688

Garfinkel, P. (2010, February 27). A family's vision. *New York Times*. Retrieved from http://www.nytimes.com/2010/02/28/jobs/28boss.html?_r=0

Garzon, J. C. (2013, July 18). What does El Salvador's homicide distribution say about the gang truce? *InSight Crime*. Retrieved from http://www.insightcrime.org/news-analysis/what-does-el-salvador-homicide-distribution-say-about-the-truce

Gini in the bottle. (2013, November 26). Democracy in America. *The Economist*. Retrieved from http://www.economist.com/blogs/democracyinamerica/2013/11/inequality-america

Gould, J. L., & Lauria-Santiago, A. A. (2008). *To rise in darkness: Revolution, repression, and memory in El Salvador, 1920–1932*. Durham, NC: Duke University Press.

Guillermoprieto, A. (2011, November 10). In the new gangland of El Salvador. *The New York Review of Books*. Retrieved from http://www.nybooks.com/articles/archives/2011/nov/10/new-gangland-el-salvador/?pagination=false

Herrmann, L. (2012, February 17). El Salvador uses failed 'iron fist' policies against rising crime. *Digital Journal*. Retrieved from http://digitaljournal.com/article/319205

Hipsman, F., & Meissner, D. (2013, April 16). Immigration in the United States: New economic, social, political landscapes with legislative reform on the horizon. *Online Journal of the Migration Policy Institute*. Retrieved from http://www.migrationpolicy.org/article/immigration-united-states-new-economic-social-political-landscapes-legislative-reform

Holder, M. D., & Coleman, B. (2009). The contribution of social relationships to children's happiness. *Journal of Happiness Studies, 10*(3), 329–349.

Immigration Policy Center. (2013). Why don't they just get in line? American Immigration Council. Retrieved from http://www.immigrationpolicy.org/just-facts/why-don%E2%80%99t-they-just-get-in-line

Index Mundi. (2009). El Salvador income distribution. Retrieved from http://www.indexmundi.com/facts/el-salvador/income-distribution

Index Mundi. (2013). El Salvador economy profile 2013. Retrieved from http://www.indexmundi.com/el_salvador/economy_profile.html

Interpeace. (2013, October 28). Interpeace hosts practice briefing on gang-truce in El Salvador. Retrieved from http://www.interpeace.org/2011-08-08-15-19-20/latest-news/474-gang-truce-el-salvador

Joint United States Government–Government of El Salvador Technical Team. (2011). *Partnership for growth: El Salvador constraints analysis.* San Salvador, El Salvador: Author. Retrieved from http://www.google.com/url?sa=t&rct=j&q=&esrc=s&source=web&cd=1&ved=0CCcQFjAA&url=http%3A%2F%2Fphotos.state.gov%2Flibraries%2Felsavador%2F92891%2FPFG%2FES%-2520Constraints_Analysis.pdf&ei=qYVdU6DBHpPwyAHDloHY-Dg&usg=AFQjCNG5nI_V4fXDd6jtPVRohP_mwqsFoQ&sig2=Yx-Qkvf-zLFFna4u0d7DTxw&bvm=bv.65397613,d.aWc

Kandel, S., & Cuéllar, N. (2011, May). *Migration, rural livelihoods and natural resource management: Lessons from El Salvador.* San Salvador, El Salvador: PRISMA Foundation. Retrieved from http://www.prisma.org.sv/index.php?id=detalle&tx_ttnews[tt_news]=331&cHash=9af711a8a4dec39201f304d514bf6c8b

Kennedy, C. (2010, April 7). Their own little haven. http://claykennedy.wordpress.com/

Kent, M. M. (2010). El Salvador survey shows lower fertility, increased contraceptive use. Population Reference Bureau. Retrieved from http://www.prb.org/Publications/Articles/2010/elsalvador.aspx

Kent, S. (2010). Symbols of love: Consumption, transnational migration, and the family in San Salvador, El Salvador. *Urban Anthropology and Studies of Cultural Systems and World Economic Development*, *39*(1/2), 73–108.

Khrais, R. (2012, September 25). Phone home: Tech draws parents, college kids closer. *NPR News Around the Nation*. Retrieved from http://www.npr.org/2012/09/25/161716306/phone-home-tech-draws-parents-college-kids-closer

Kozol, J. (2000). *Ordinary Resurrections: Children in the Years of Hope*. New York: Crown Publishers.

Larson, R., & Wilson, S. (2004). Globalization and the changing pathways to adulthood. In R. M. Lerner & L. Steinberg (Eds.), *Handbook of adolescent psychology* (2nd ed), (pp. 299–331). New York: Wiley.

Left turn: El Salvador's presidential election. (2009, March 21). *The Economist* 390.8623 (p. 40). Retrieved from http://www.economist.com/node/13331169

Leung, A., Kier, C., Fung, T., Fung, L., & Sproule, R. (2011). Searching for happiness: The importance of social capital. *Journal of Happiness Studies 12*(3), 443–462.

Levitt, P. & Schiller, N. G. (2004). Conceptualizing simultaneity: A transnational social field perspective on society (p. 1028). *International Migration Review*, *38*(3), 1002–1039.

Lindo-Fuentes, H. (2008). Schooling in El Salvador. In S. Gvirtz & J. Beech (Eds.), *Going to school in Latin America* (pp. 179–202). Westport, CT: Greenwood Press.

Looft, C. (2012, June 18). El Salvador police use uniforms to distinguish jailed members of rival gangs. *InSight Crime*. Retrieved from http://www.insightcrime.org/insight-latest-news/item/2783-el-salvador-police-give-uniforms-to-jailed-gang-members

López, K. (2011, October 3). 90% de las remesas se gasta en consumo. *La Prensa Grafica*. Retrieved from http://www.laprensagrafica.com/economia/nacional/221436-90-de-las-remesas-se-gasta-en-consumo

López, T. (2012, November 24). Ninis – A generation that neither works, nor studies in El Salvador. *Fox News Latino*. Retrieved from http://latino.foxnews.com/latino/lifestyle/2012/11/24/ninis-generation-that-neither-works-nor-studies-in-el-salvador/#ixzz2Z21g4hpY

Lottery of Life. (2012, November 21). *The Economist*. Retrieved from http://www.economist.com/news/21566430-where-be-born-2013-lottery-life

Macabasco, L. W. (2006, March 3). The train of death: Migrants riding freights north from Central America risk their lives to reach the U.S. *Mother Jones*. Retrieved from http://www.motherjones.com/politics/2006/03/train-death?page=2

Marcin, J. D. (2013). Migrant workers' remittances, citizenship, and the state: The case of El Salvador. *Harvard Civil Rights-Civil Liberties Law Review, 48*(2), 531–551.

Massey, D., Durand, J., & Malone, N. J. (2002). *Beyond smoke and mirrors: Mexican immigration in an era of economic integration* (p. 20). New York: Russell Sage Foundation.

Meissner, D., Kerwin, D. M., Chishti, M., & Bergeron, C. (2013). *Immigration enforcement in the United States: The rise of a formidable machinery*. Washington, DC: Migration Policy Institute.

Merton, R. K. (1936). The unanticipated consequences of purposive social action. *American Sociological Review 1*(6): 895.

Meyer, P. J., & Sullivan, M. P. (2012, June 26). U.S. foreign assistance to Latin America and the Caribbean: Recent trends and FY2013 appropriations. Washington, DC: Congressional Research Service.

Mills, F. B. (2012, March 5). Education reform gets high marks in El Salvador. Council on Hemispheric Relations. Retrieved from http://www.coha.org/education-reform-gets-high-marks-in-el-salvador/

Mistral, G. (1933, September 2). El Salvador. *Repertorio Americano XXVII*: 9.

Moodie, E. (2010). *El Salvador in the aftermath of peace: Crime, uncertainty, and the transition to democracy* (pp. 93-95). Philadelphia: University of Pennsylvania Press.

Morán, G. (2013, July 12). Una de cada cinco niñas en áreas empobrecidas es madre antes de los 15. *ContraPunto*. Retrieved from http://www.contrapunto.com.sv/genero/una-de-cada-cinco-ninas-en-areas-empobrecidas-es-madre-antes-de-los-15

Muth, T. (2010, November 30). The Central Reserve Bank and Burger King. Retrieved from Tim's El Salvador Blog, http://luterano.blogspot.com/2010/11/central-reserve-bank-and-burger-king.html

Muth, T. (2013, July 18). Looking at where murders happen. Retrieved from Tim's El Salvador Blog, http://luterano.blogspot.com/2013/07/looking-at-where-murders-happen.html

Muth, T. (2013, December 29). Volcanic ash cloud from San Miguel volcano. Retrieved from Tim's El Salvador Blog, http://luterano.blogspot.com/search?q=volcanic+ash

National Oceanic and Atmospheric Association. (2009, January 23). Mitch: The deadliest Atlantic hurricane since 1780. Retrieved from http://www.ncdc.noaa.gov/oa/reports/mitch/mitch.html

National Research Council. (2005). *Growing up global: The changing transitions to adulthood in developing countries*. Washington, DC: The National Academies Press.

Nazario, S. (2006). *Enrique's Journey*. New York: Random House.

Nightingale, D. S., & Wandner, S. A. (2011, August). Informal and nonstandard employment in the United States: Implications for low-income working families. Washington, DC: The Urban Institute. Retrieved from http://www.urban.org

Nordland, R. (1984, March 23). How 2 rose to vie for El Salvador's presidency. *Philadelphia Inquirer*: A1.

Orozco, M. (2006). *Transnational families: Lives on the edge, but in pursuit of change* (p. 2). Washington, DC: Georgetown University Institute for the Study of International Migration (ISIM).

Parkinson, C. (2014, January 21). El Salvador bus extortion doubles to $36 mn amid failing gang truce. *InSight Crime*. Retrieved from http://www.insightcrime.org/news-briefs/el-salvador-annual-bus-extortion-doubles-to-$36-mn-amid-failing-gang-truce

Parreñas, R. S. (2005). *Children of global migration: Transnational families and gendered woes*. Stanford, CA: Stanford University Press.

Pearson, E. (2013, April 9). Pregnant woman kidnapped and tortured as she immigrated to U.S. *New York Daily News*. Retrieved from http://www.nydailynews.com/new-york/citizenship-now/pregnant-woman-kidnapped-tortured-immigrating-u-s-article-1.1312307#ixzz2Rm8cbWUE

Penhaul, K. (2010, June 25). 'Train of death' drives migrant American dreamers. *CNN*. Retrieved from http://edition.cnn.com/2010/WORLD/americas/06/23/mexico.train.death/index.html

Perla, H., Jr., & Cruz-Feliciano, H. (2013). The twenty-first-century left in El Salvador and Nicaragua: Understanding apparent contradictions and criticisms. *Latin American Perspectives 40*(3), 83–106.

Pew Research Hispanic Trends Project. (2013, January 29). A nation of immigrants: A portrait of the 40 million, including 11 million unauthorized. Retrieved from http://www.pewhispanic.org/2013/01/29/a-nation-of-immigrants/

Portes, A. (2008, July 1). Migration and social change: Some conceptual reflections. Keynote address to the conference "Theorizing Key Migration Debates." Oxford University. Retrieved from http://www.imi.ox.ac.uk/pdfs/alejandro-portes-migration-and-social-change-some-conceptual-reflections/view

Quintana, V., & Winship, J. (2010). *Migracion: Juventud ojos abiertos en El Salvador (Migration: Youth with their Eyes Wide Open in El Salvador)*. San Salvador, El Salvador: Universidad Panamericana.

Quintana, V., & Winship, J. (2011). *Migración proyectos de vida, mujeres jóvenes en El Salvador (Migration and Life Plans for Young Women in El Salvador)* San Salvador, El Salvador: Universidad Panamericana.

Ramos, C. G. (2011). *Identidades, practicas, y expectivas juveniles: Al inicio del Siglo XXI*. San Salvador: FLACSO—Programa El Salvador.

Ramsey, G. (2012, February 23). How insecurity taints "Latin America's decade." *InSight Crime*. Retrieved from http://www.insightcrime. org/news-analysis/how-insecurity-taints-latin-americas-decade

Ratha, D., Eigen-Zucchi, C., Plaza, S., Wyss, H., & Yi, S. (2013, October 2). *Migration and development brief 21*. Washington, DC: World Bank. Retrieved from http://econ. worldbank.org/WBSITE/EXTERNAL/EXTDEC/EXTDEC-PROSPECTS/0,,contentMDK:21125572~pagePK:64165401~piP-K:64165026~theSitePK:476883,00.html

Reagan, R. (1984, May 9). Address to the nation on United States policy in Central America. Retrieved from http://www.reagan.utexas. edu/archives/speeches/1984/50984h.htm

Rice, M. (2010, June 4). Not everyone wants to live in America. *Forbes*. Retrieved from http://www.forbes.com/2010/06/04/immigration-emigration-expats-opinions-contributors-mark-rice.html

Rojas-Flores, L., Herrera, S., Currier, J. M., Lin, E. Y., Kulzer, R., & Foy, D. W. (2013). "We are raising our children in fear": War, community violence, and parenting practices in El Salvador. *International Perspectives in Psychology: Research, Practice, Consultation, 2*(4), 269–285.

Ross, L. (1977). The intuitive psychologist and his shortcomings: Distortions in the attribution process. In L. Berkowitz (Ed.), *Advances in experimental social psychology* (Vol. 10) (pp. 173–220). New York: Academic Press.

Rubin, J. (2004). El Salvador: Payback. Public Broadcasting System Frontline World. Retrieved from http://www.pbs.org/frontlineworld/elections/elsalvador/

Salas-Wright, C.P., Olate, R., & Vaughn, M. (2013). Religious coping, spirituality, and substance use and abuse among youth in high-risk communities in San Salvador, El Salvador. *Substance Use and Misuse,* 48(9), 769–783.

Samuelson, R. J. (2012, December 9). Is the economy creating a lost generation? *The Washington Post: Opinions.* Retrieved from http://www.washingtonpost.com/opinions/robert-samuelson-is-the-economy-creating-a-lost-generation/2012/12/09/41683956-4093-11e2-bca3-aadc9b7e29c5_story.html

Santacruz Giralt, M., & Carranza, M. (2009). *Encuesta nacional de juventud: Analisis de resultados.* San Salvador: Instituto Universitario de Opinion Publica, Universidad Centroamerican "José Simeón Cañas."

Santos, J. (2013, May 25). 470,264 personas afines a pandillas. *La Prensa Grafica.* Retrieved from http://www.laprensagrafica.com/470-264-personas-afines-a-pandillas

Saunders, R., Rivas, F., Rabossi, M., Mercedes Ruiz, A., Avanzini, D., & Helwig, J. (2012, January). *El Salvador: Higher education assessment and recommendations.* San Salvador, El Salvador: United States Agency for International Development (USAID). Retrieved from http://www.gem2.org/node/139

Seelke, C. R. (2012, November 9). *El Salvador: Political and economic conditions and U.S. relations.* Report to Congress 7-5700. Washington, DC: Congressional Research Service. Retrieved from https://opencrs.com/document/RS21655/

Silva Ávalos, H. (2014, March 1). Corruption in El Salvador: Politicians, police, and transportistas. *CLALS Working Paper Series No. 4.* Retrieved from http://papers.ssrn.com/sol3/papers.cfm?abstract_id=2419174

SITEAL (Sistema de Información de Tendencias Educativas en América Latina) (2012). *El Salvador en contexto*. Retrieved from http://www.siteal.iipe-oei.org/sites/default/files/perfil_el_salvador_2013_06.pdf

Tegel, S. (2012, July 17). El Salvador: 'How long until the waves reach us?'. Retrieved from http://www.globalpost.com/dispatch/news/regions/americas/120714/el-salvador-climate-change-rising-sea-level

Thompson, G., & Cohen, S. (2014, April 6). More deportations follow minor crimes, records show. *The New York Times*. Retrieved from http://www.nytimes.com/2014/04/07/us/more-deportations-follow-minor-crimes-data-shows.html?_r=0

UNESCO. (2009). *Global monitoring report 2009: Overcoming inequality: Why governance matters*. Oxford: UNESCO.

United Nations Development Program. (2005). *A look at the new 'us': The impact of migrations*. San Salvador, El Salvador: Author.

United Nations Development Program. (2011). *Human development report 2011, Sustainability and equity: A better future for all*. New York: Author.

United Nations Development Program. (2013). *Informe sobre Desarrollo Humano El Salvador 2013*. San Salvador, El Salvador: Author. Retrieved from http://www.sv.undp.org/content/el_salvador/es/home/library/poverty/informe-sobre-desarrollo-humano-el-salvador-2013/

United Nations Office on Drugs and Crime. (2014). Global Study on Homicide. Retrieved from https://www.unodc.org/gsh/en/data.html

United Nations Security Council. (1993). *Report of the Truth Commission in El Salvador—From madness to hope: The 12-year war in El Salvador*. Retrieved from http://www.derechos.org/nizkor/salvador/informes/truth.html

United Nations University. (2012, October 23). Our world at risk: A look at *WorldRiskReport 2012*. Retrieved from http://unu.edu/publications/articles/our-world-at-risk.html

United States Bureau of Citizenship and Immigration Services. (2000, October 16). *El Salvador: The role of ORDEN in the El Salvadoran civil war*, SLV01001.ZAR. Retrieved from http://www.refworld.org/docid/3dee04524.html

United States Department of Commerce Bureau of Economic Analysis. (2014). Gross domestic product (GDP) by industry data. Retrieved from http://www.bea.gov/industry/gdpbyind_data.htm

United States Department of State. (2011). Country reports on human rights practices for 2011: El Salvador. Retrieved from http://www.state.gov/j/drl/rls/hrrpt/humanrightsreport/index.htm?dlid=186513

Voices on the Border: Information and Analysis from El Salvador. (2011, February 15). Unemployment in El Salvador. [Weblog]. Retrieved from http://voiceselsalvador.wordpress.com/2011/02/15/unemployment-in-el-salvador/

Watts, D. J. (2004). *Six degrees: The science of a connected age* (p. 283). New York: W. W. Norton.

Wearden, G. (2013, November 29). Eurozone youth unemployment hits record high; Netherlands downgraded – as it happened. *Guardian.com*. Retrieved from http://www.theguardian.com/business/2013/nov/29/netherlands-loses-aaa-rating-eurozone-unemployment-live#-block-529869e0e4b09ac370af286c

Whedon, J. (2013). Commencement speech. *The Wesleyan Connection*. Retrieved from https://newsletter.blogs.wesleyan.edu/2013/05/26/whedoncommencement/

Wiltberger, J. (2009). Bringing Latin America into US debates on Latino immigration: Views from El Salvador. *Development 52*(4), 519–524.

Winship, J. & Quintana, V. (2005). *Una familia, dos paises (One family, two countries: Understanding the impact on youth when their parent(s) emigrate to the United States)*. San Salvador, El Salvador: Universidad Panamericana.

Wohletz, K. H. (2000). Were the Dark Ages triggered by volcano-related climate changes in the 6th century? *EOS, Transactions, American Geophysical Union, 48*(81), F1305.

World Bank. (2014). GNI per capita, Atlas method (current US$). Retrieved from http://data.worldbank.org/indicator/NY.GNP.PCAP.CD

Zilberg, E., & Lungo, M. (1999). 'Se han vuelto haraganes': Jovenes salvadoreños, migración y identitades laborales. In M. Lungo & S. Kandell (Eds.), *Transformado El Salvador: Migración, sociedad, y cultura* (pp. 39–93). San Salvador: Fundación Nacional para el Desarrollo.

Index

41140775R00131

Made in the USA
Lexington, KY
30 April 2015